COMMUNICATION AS
COMMITMENT

Communication as Commitment

HARRY DeWIRE

FORTRESS PRESS
Philadelphia

Library of Congress Catalog Card Number 70–171497

ISBN 0–8006–0104–1

1873G71   Printed in the United States of America   1–104

CONTENTS

FOREWORD

"Where there is communication there is hope," says President Kenneth Kaunda of Zambia in Central Africa. Africans are experts in interpersonal relations. And this is the wisdom of demonstrated authority.

Harry DeWire has demonstrated his authority in the area under discussion as professor of psychology and pastoral care at United Theological Seminary, Dayton, Ohio, through numerous journal articles, and especially in his important book *The Christian as Communicator* (Philadelphia: Westminster Press, 1960). It is highly appropriate that a decade later he should offer to a wider audience the essence of his heightened expertise and deepened insights in the present volume.

Seldom have the will and the skill to communicate been more sorely needed than in the tensions that characterize church and society in contemporary America, with its widening gulf between traditionalists and progressives, old and young, whites and minorities, men and women, "eggheads" and hardhats.

The philosophical dualism that Western Christianity inherited from ancient Greece is one factor that makes us particularly prone to polarization. People tend to think in terms of either-or rather than both-and. Furthermore, polarization often takes place in times of accelerating social change, with its accompanying dislocation and insecurity. People become frightened. Some want to protect their own possessions and social standing, and the traditional values that support these. They are ready to be ruthless in their defense. Others are sure that inherited structures of society and church are beyond salvage. They are persuaded that their own ideas alone will lead to a future of human well-being and security. And they are prepared to be equally merciless.

In this anguished dilemma the present contribution by Professor DeWire is particularly well timed. Pastors, church workers, and lay Christians, whatever their personal tendencies or sympathies, will find valuable help in developing their motivation and their abilities to communicate with other persons. The health of the individual, the family, society, and the church depends on improved communication.

WILLIAM J. DANKER
Editor, Church-in-Mission Series

INTRODUCTION

Communication and *commitment* are familiar terms in the language of the Christian faith, but we usually think of them as separate aspects of human experience. The purpose of this book is to deal with both of them as one experience. Commitment is a form of inner dialogue governed by all the laws of communication. Communication with others is but an extension of this inner dialogue, and thus it becomes a commitment to others. The goal of this commitment in the Christian's context is to maintain and develop a community of thought and action based upon the will and work of God's spirit. Communication defined in this way is, in a sense, a reflection upon and evaluation of ourselves. No longer is it enough to ask, "Did I say the right thing?" We must deal with our meanings, the filters through which the meanings must pass, the "feedback" from others, the subtleties and refinements of language and gesture, and the art of listening. For the most part, the church has focused its efforts in two directions: toward the use of mass media and toward the development of small group interaction. Less attention has been given to the individual in his daily life. How does he form his commitments and carry them out as he relates to people? Each normal person is a self-contained communication system with all the capacities and energies required for effective encounter with the world. The ability to engage in the delicate exchange of meaning and thought makes the individual a significant factor in the growth of the community of God's people. The individual Christian can be either active or reflective, intimate with others or alone, rooted in a restricted community or mobile. His numerous day-by-day contacts offer him an unlimited opportunity to develop his communication skills.

These chapters will deal with the more important aspects of one-to-one communication. They will look first at the inner dialogue, the intrapersonal source of commitment, and then follow this commitment into relationships with the world.

The material for the book .was presented to a conference of ministers at Concordia Seminary, Saint Louis, in the summer of 1968. Dr. William Danker of the Concordia faculty has given helpful suggestions and encouragement to proceed with the publication of the lectures.

Chapter I

INTRAPERSONAL
DIALOGUE

Of all the characteristics of human life, the most vexing and at the same time the most rewarding is our ability to communicate. We know that many of the crises of life are caused by the breakdown of communication. In such crises our feelings are aroused, but we cannot find words to express them. Misunderstandings between individuals, groups, and cultures continue because we lack proper channels of communication. We cannot function as individuals or as a society without the communication of symbolic behavior. Providing food, shelter, and entertainment would be impossible without the use of language, gesture, signs, and the complex media through which persons send and receive messages.

To some extent, we are perplexed because we cannot define what we mean by communication. In a sense we do know what it is and recognize it when it occurs, and most of the time we are at ease while participating in it. We use the term freely, even to the point of making value judgments about it; it "breaks down," "moves along easily," "takes place at deep levels," we say. It is one thing to be able to describe how communication is carried on, however, and quite another to describe what is actually taking place. In this respect it resembles our understanding of the term *space*. It can be measured, occupied, decorated, darkened, and otherwise understood through the senses. But we cannot know what it is. In discussing such terms we must say, with Saint Augustine, "I know so long as you don't ask me."

If communication cannot be defined, we are at least learning more and more about it by trying to describe how it takes place. But here again we run into difficulty because the task is enormous and requires a knowledge of a great many fields of interest. If an exhaustive study were to be made of the entire human communication system, it would have to include findings from psychology, anthropology, sociology, linguistics, theology, philosophy, engineering, physiology, and mathematics. All these fields have developed theories of communication within their separate disciplines. In fact, it has been suggested that the study of communication has become so universal that it might well serve as the common basis for the interchange of ideas and findings among the academic disciplines. In some fields (especially linguistics, mathematics, and engineering) theory has been reduced to statistical and mathematical formulas to describe the use of signs, words, and channels of communication. These aspects of human expression are measurable and even predictable. They are apt to remain constant in all situations, and it is this constancy that makes possible the languages and codes by which we live. Moreover, even though we are perplexed by the process of communication, we are not unaware of what the discoveries about communication have done to us. Electronic and mechanical inventions have brought about radical changes in our methods of conversation, learning, and passing along information.

In more primitive societies the means and methods of communication were (and are) confined to the rather simple matter of individual contact. With few exceptions (beating drums, smoke signals) this type of society depended upon the primary communication skills to sustain it. The individual was involved firsthand and was required to confront others with his entire person. If he chose to mask his feelings or obscure his meanings, he could not hide behind a printed message or an electronic device.

Not long ago I had my first experience in bargaining with a West African trader for an ebony carving I wanted to buy. Even after being warned that I was expected to haggle with him about the price, I was not quite prepared for the sharp personal interchange required of me. He was neither ashamed to admit that he was asking too much nor reluctant to groan and complain about my tightfisted ways. More important, he soon taught *me* how to groan and complain about the proceedings. Admittedly, this was all a rather refined and time-tested method of barter, but how different from paying the price marked on the tag and picking up your change from a little dish. In our society buying and selling and countless other human transactions can be accomplished without any significant human encounter.

Communication is not a *single* happening, but rather a *series* of happenings involving two or more persons. To be complete, the series must produce a cycle of occurrences which require the participants to engage in all component parts of the process: sensing, response, speaking, listening, evaluation, and reflection. The only human event in which this process can occur demands the physical presence of the participants. If any of the component parts are missing or inadequately employed, the communication process will, to that extent, be disturbed.

In mass communication the steps in the cycle are either weakened or excluded by distance, by the intervention of technology, and by the inability of the person to evaluate or respond adequately. The communication of the deepest spiritual meanings requires the use of all the steps in the process, and it is the purpose of these chapters to show how intimate, face-to-face encounter becomes the ultimate means by which persons develop an understanding of their spiritual nature and commit themselves to the expression of that nature.

I

Communication originates as a response to the constant barrage of stimuli reaching our senses. Some of these stimuli originate in our surroundings; others, within ourselves. Whatever their origin, we are bound to respond. Even our attempts to be indifferent to such stimuli or to avoid them are actually responses of a sort. A stimulating situation nudges into action a series of mental and emotional processes that usually results in some form of physical expression. If this activity occurs while someone is paying attention to us, his reaction makes use of the same processes. Of all the steps in this series of activities, the most visible is the way we signal each other by sound and gesture. However, before communication reaches the point of expression, it must filter through (1) the meanings we associate with life, (2) our characteristic emotional responses to life, and (3) the selection of an appropriate means of translating the meanings into action.

It is within this series of human activities that we transact our spiritual affairs. If we understand communication broadly enough to reach down into the meanings we give to life, we are then dealing with spiritual commitment. In some respects the term *commitment* (from the Latin for "to connect or to send with") more nearly describes the process we are talking about than does the term *communication* (from the French "to put in common"). All human action is commitment to something, to ourselves or to love for God and for others. Communication, then, is our spiritual commitment, the witness to our understanding of the will of God. It is man's mode of "being-in-the-world." It is his attempt to master and influence the everyday give-and-take with his fellowman as well as the present tragic circumstances he has created for himself—religious disputes, overpopulation, atomic threat, and the persistent tensions between races and nations.

To understand man's "being-in-the-world" we could begin at almost any point along the communication process and move in either direction, from meaning to expression or from expression to meaning. We will begin with meaning, since this level is most readily affected when we are aroused to action.

In the first place, when aroused by some stimulus we are made conscious of ourselves and of all the presuppositions we make about ourselves. We are self-observers, and we literally talk to ourselves about what we see and feel. We correct our mistakes, improve our state of mind, evaluate our status before the world. Gradually, through childhood and adolescence, we develop a self-regarding motif. We learn how to judge our behavior and correct our errors. If we are loved, we learn eventually that love is a part of our own life. We do not depend upon another to make it happen. Love governs our actions and influences our perception of the world. When we react critically to the world, the knowledge of a loving God is neither strange nor unacceptable. The spirit of Christ makes sense to feelings already understood. We are in possession of the equipment for wholesome self-perception.

If love is a part of our inner life, it is because this is how we have been created. To be sure, we must learn how to accept and express love, but love is a favor from God. If we become loving persons, it is only because we have found

5

the source and meaning of life. It constantly bids to become a part of our self-awareness.

The inner world of goal-setting, decision-making, and imagination is actually a form of *intrapersonal* communication.[1] The behavioral scientists have long debated over how man's mind obtains the data from which it formulates ideas and plans of action. At one extreme are those who insist that the mind is passive, going into action only when stimulated by the senses. In other words, the mind has no mind of its own. It is reactive and incapable of creating ideas or notions without some stimulus from the outside. To these scientists, the external and visible environment is more important than what happens inside the mind.

At the other extreme are those who hold that the mind is much more than reactive. It is the *source* of creating, desiring, pondering, promoting, defending. The mind is full of sensations created only by itself and dealt with only by itself. It is, in a sense, a self-contained sphere of communication, an occurrence within the mind that needs only the active reflection upon and struggle between elements that often are in conflict. These elements communicate with each other. Because the place of origin and the destination of the message are wholly within the soul of the individual, this is sometimes referred to as *intrapersonal* communication.

This internal conversation may become very specific, but the basic elements generally remain the same. One element in the conversation is the love of God, urging us toward self-fulfillment and personal harmony with the source of our existence. The other element is the knowledge of our solitariness in the world, and our need for self-enhance-

1. The term was used by Ruesch and Bateson to describe the process of self-observation by which a person obtains insight into his own culture. See Jürgen Ruesch and Gregory Bateson, *Communication: The Social Matrix of Psychiatry* (New York: W. W. Norton, 1951), pp. 199 ff.

ment and acceptance. The conversation between them is not always simple dialogue. More often than not, intrapersonal communication is conflict and struggle. God's love, we feel, cannot solve many of the pressures of competition, social survival, and even moral expectancy. Yet, the love of God persists, never letting the inner conversation take place without demanding a hearing.

It is likely that more people than we imagine feel the tensions of this inner dialogue. Some think that people do not know how to love, but the possibility is that they do not recognize the context in which love operates. The "I and thou" relationship which is essential to that context begins within the person. Science possesses instruments sufficient only to study the "I" and its functions. The vast literature dealing with human behavior, both scientific and popular, has encouraged us to seek the causes of and solutions for our difficulties within the observable data of human life. If we are hostile, the blame is laid at the feet of rejecting adults or peers. If we are open, tender, and loving in our human relationships, credit must be given to those who shaped the "I" during childhood. Throughout life we may try to find the secret to our behavior by adjusting and rearranging the emotional and mental processes we interpret to be the "I."

A growing number of psychologists recognize that the problem of the self contains an enigma not wholly solved by the accepted methods of the study of human behavior. Gordon Allport says, "The subject opens up profound philosophical dilemmas concerning the nature of man, of 'soul,' of freedom and immortality. It is easy to see why many psychological discussions of personality avoid the problem altogether."[2] To solve the enigma, we must rely upon our knowledge of and faith in God's action in creat-

2. Gordon Allport, *Pattern and Growth in Personality* (New York: Holt, Rinehart and Winston, 1961), p. 111.

ing man. Communion with God is not an option for man. Man is made for communion with God just as he is made to reason with his fellows.

II

*Intra*personal communication (the encounter within) and *inter*personal communication (the encounter with others) seem to be governed by identical principles. The entire series of events in the communication process reflects a specific style of life. While there are numerous types of people with many ways of expressing themselves, there are only two options for our behavior as communicators. We are either "immune" to the *other* in the process, or we "commune" with him.

To be immune is to be guarded, protected, neither susceptible nor responsive. For our physical health it is a blessing. For our human relationships, as well as our relation to God, it is a frustrating and disturbing style of life. For the immune person, the field of action within himself is confined to his own resources. He does not respond to the urge to search for the wisdom and love of God. He trusts only himself and believes that all answers lie within his power to protect and defend what is his and what he believes. He forces himself to play at "being God" and thereby develops an inordinate pride in who he is and what he does.

Immunity to the love of God within ourselves will cause us to be immune to other people. We move into the world without trust, except in those people and situations that clearly reflect our interests and feelings. Much of the world is alien to us. We become insensitive to the way God is working among people because we are insensitive to the activity of God in our own lives. We judge people and events by our own standards, and in the presence of new and creative opportunities for life and action we feel alone and insecure.

To commune with another is to share a common experience, that is, an experience of "commonness." For our inner life this means considerably more than "talking" to God or trying to break through some kind of barrier to get a hearing from God. It means what the gospel has taught us: that God shares our life with us. He struggles in our struggles, rejoices in our joy. We become great persons because we are in God, but he also becomes something because he is in us: "For God is at work in you, both to will and to work for his good pleasure" (Philippians 2:13). To commune with God is to accept his life as a part of our life, to have faith in his love and wish for our happiness. Our style of life is marked by openness and search.

Sharing a common experience with God gives us a spirit of community in the world. We see other people as children of God who can share a common life. We can love our neighbor because we see him as someone who is exactly like ourselves. Instead of protecting what we are, we do not fear to open ourselves to others. God is among us, opening the possibility for the expression of community.

There can be no question about the effect of early training and conditioning in creating an immunity to love. Before the child is conscious of himself as a unique and separate entity, he probably makes no distinction between the environment and himself. (Of course, the experience of birth is a significant separation of the child from his mother, and it is hard to overestimate the degree of impoverishment he suffers if he has inadequate care and protection.) However, within a few months, the person begins a series of separation experiences lasting the rest of his life.

The first of these is the development of awareness, the discovery that the environment is separate and different from himself. Immediately he has to mobilize his inner resources for independent living. By means of repeated experimenting with his separateness, alternating with frequent and rewarding return to parental love, he learns to trust what is inside himself. But, if his independent action does not bring corresponding experiences of emotional sheltering and comfort, the person does *not* learn to trust himself. He is unsure of his actions, unable to understand the full range of his powers. He only knows *he must protect himself.* If these experiences are reinforced by additional and persistent frustrations, he is well on the way to a style of life characterized by immunity to love.

There are numerous ways in which such a person addresses himself to the world, none of them truly communicative. He may distrust the intentions of others and respond with the only defense he knows: argument and debate. Or his distrust may go to the level of fear, causing him to escape encounter whenever possible. Another possible reaction is the effort to cling to whoever and whatever give him some assurance of selfhood and a feeling of comfort. For this person, certain other persons and certain ideas are not easily surrendered. His mind cannot change; and usually it is insensitive to new persons or new ideas. The immune person confronts his world with only his own resources.

At the other extreme, commitment to (contact with) the source of love permits easy and free movement within the world. But the achievement of this ability depends upon the nature of the commitment and how far it goes. Separation from parents, loving though they may be, does not always automatically guarantee the discovery of God. Even in those instances where God does take over, the result may be a God created by the person to be just a larger and more divine parent. Such a God "tells" him what to do, gives him comfort, and offers protection. Or a man may venture to take the mantle of God upon himself. To protect himself against isolation, he acts the part of God, telling himself he is right and being constantly alert to wrongness in others.

It is exactly at this point that the study of communication as a spiritual phenomenon is most frustrated. We need to know what takes place within the person to cause him to express himself the way he does. What precedes his speech? Why is he sometimes immune to people and at other times in communication with them? How does he become consistently committed to love in his relationships? The answers lie in at least four elements that seem to combine to produce effective and creative expression in the presence of others. All of them are rooted in man's ability and need to see, to be curious, and to explore. Two are described here and the others will be discussed in the next chapter.

1. Sometimes our world is referred to as a field or an arena of action. This field contains all the elements about which we have some knowledge and with which we have some relationship. The rapid growth of our means of keeping up with the events of men and nations has enlarged our field to the point where it overwhelms us. But this is our given situation. We might wish the world to be different or refuse to admit that it is so complex and demanding, but we have it just as it is. If we try to commit ourselves to a world other than the one we are in, our communication will certainly miss the mark. God is in the world as it is and not as we want it to be. The ability to see him there is the first step toward spiritual commitment.

There might be some question about which comes first in human growth, our ability to see God at work in his world or at work in ourselves. It would seem, however, that we can learn much about God and our status before him if our perception of the world is realistic and our judgments about it are honest. We cannot always make correct judgments, because the number of things to be interpreted

11

is too great for us. Nor can we be satisfied with public or private opinion, for God has a way of working in hidden and remote events of our history. We must search for love, humility, and peace, which means that we must consider all persons to be part of our world. These traits, however hidden, reside in all of us. Our commitment is to the world, not to selected parts of it. Without this breadth of field, we cannot know the full range of God's love.

Our judgments about the world can be made only as a part of our intrapersonal communication. The decision to make these judgments honestly and deliberately is the first struggle in our commitment to God. We will find in ourselves what we find in the world. The struggles and sins of all mankind are found in the single person, and it is only in this community of human alikeness that communication is possible.

2. The second element needed to develop our intrapersonal skills moves us from the general to the specifics of our world. We do not think about or judge individuals as we do people in general. In fact, studies have shown that some people who are good judges of "the public" are not necessarily good judges of "the person." The clergyman might be readily convinced that the congregation appreciated his sermon, but not be able to estimate the nature of that appreciation in a single parishioner. Understanding the individual person, however, is vital to our self-understanding.

Everyone has had the experience of hitting it off with another person at first sight. Similarity of interests often draws us to one another. It is the things we have in common that permit us to reach one another and maintain relationships. Yet all too often we use our similarities as a means of staying at arm's length from others. As long as we can share similar complaints, the events of daily life, and the opinions we hold in common, we protect ourselves from discovering meanings. Such a relationship is especially inviting to the immune person, since he is required neither to betray the insecurities of his inner life nor to become involved in the meanings of the other.

But it is exactly this process that can deepen the understanding of our inner nature and open us to the will of God. If we can permit our encounter with another to explore the level of meaning, we will find that the similarity of goals, purpose, and values is common to all men, whereas our similarity of race, creed, or even interests divides us into groups that build barriers out of those similarities. We are more nearly alike than we want to believe. To engage other persons at the level where they feel, think, plan, and perceive is to stimulate us to engage ourselves at that same level.

There is reason to doubt that we can correct and improve our inner lives all by ourselves. While it may seem that God comes to us directly to show us where we are wrong, it cannot be denied that the experience of the wrong usually comes from our contact with others. Suppose two persons are working to prepare a church budget for the year. Both of them come with some notion as to how it should be done and what it should contain. These notions grow not only out of their knowledge of budget-making but also out of their life-style. Sam tends to be passive and accommodating. He likes to be approved of by people, even at the expense of his own feelings and thoughts. By making as few changes as possible he prevents argument, especially if he is involved in it. George is a boat-rocker. He is apt to suggest change even at the expense of reason. He has strong and sometimes well-founded beliefs, but his need to dominate builds up hostility toward his beliefs.

Their meeting together starts off innocently enough, but soon runs into difficulty when George suggests they insert an item for enough money to equip a vacant lot as a playground for the children in the community. Sam is not opposed to the idea in principle, but he doesn't want to defend something that wasn't in the budget last year. The idea is new ground on which he feels uncomfortable. George wants to plunge ahead. Sam's resistance meets George's determination. Sam has to weigh George's disapproval against the disapproval of the people who will receive the report. Finally, he lets George have his way, but makes George promise that in the meeting it will be made clear that the whole idea came from George, not Sam.

Now let's follow them home. Sam feels good about the whole thing, even congratulates himself. George got what he wanted, and the board will not hold him responsible for George's wild ideas. The whole matter is dismissed from Sam's mind. But George cannot forget so easily. He knows it is Sam's nature to be afraid and cautious. He also knows of his own tendency to dominate and control. He begins to wonder about his behavior. Was he too demanding? Did he get his own way at the expense of a relationship? If he had been more patient, he and Sam might have stood together in this thing. As it is, their relationship has actually been broken. Of course they are not enemies, but neither have they really accomplished anything together.

George realizes he has been put in the wrong by his environment. Now he faces the internal problem of recognizing mistakes and the necessity of correcting them. The only way he can handle the problem is within the framework of inner commitment. New information about himself is being understood. Open and free conversation within himself can achieve a change, not only in his actions, but also in the basic processes of his life. He is in a favorable position to opt for the establishment of a clearer sense of community in his own life and a corresponding improvement in his ability to communicate.

This process of viewing our own actions and correcting our mistakes can be guided and encouraged. It would seem, then, that preaching, teaching, pastoral ministries, and supervision within the church should result in the change of inner meanings. Each of these functions is by nature assertive. To preach or teach is to take some initiative and provide direction for the thinking of other people. Supervision of the life of the church presupposes planning and suggesting. Pastoral care is the task of moving toward people with the desire to help. But the effectiveness of these functions is not measured by the skill with which the aggression is carried through. Only when the participants withdraw from the relationship and carry on an inner conversation about the meaning of what they have been through will the result of the communication be known.

For all of us the alternation between assertiveness and withdrawal offers the dual encounter necessary to our understanding of the will of God. Even the mystic cannot shut out his environment; he simply chooses (and usually restricts) the environment to carry on this process. Some persons of individual piety try to go the mystic one better by convincing themselves that commitment to God is independent of others; that there is a Self within the self that operates without regard to our mistakes in communication. Paul comes directly to the point when he says, "It is the Spirit himself bearing witness with our spirit" (Romans 8:16). And without a spirit of our own, shaped by the give-and-take with others, the spirit of God falls on barren ground.

Every encounter with people is a risk. We must learn to tolerate being exposed to our weakness and to the need for change. We are required to let others open us to ourselves by including them in our search for meaning. When persons together engage in this process, each becomes a reality

15

to the life of the other in what Martin Buber calls "the mutual experiences of inclusion." This is a great deal more than a show of fellowship or even a unified group endeavor. It is the willingness to take the other one with us as part of our spirit. As God's spirit enlightens this "inclusion" we know what we are and what we must become.

Chapter II

COMMUNICATION
AND WITNESS

Commitment to the will of God provides us with the most accurate picture of our world and the people in it. If intrapersonal dialogue is an adventure within the will of God, we will be free to perceive the world and its people in a free and open perspective, free from threat and open to all people. But before we talk about engaging others in interpersonal communication, two additional events which occur within ourselves must be discussed.

First, by our contact with the world we develop an inner knowledge of who we are. We gain an "in-sight" about our "being-in-the-world." To know who we are is a spiritual endeavor of inner enlightenment. Second, all encounter with life develops a pressure for action. Because we are created as acting and expressive beings, we find it necessary to witness. The biblical injunction to teach, preach, and make disciples is not optional. We are bound to do it for some cause or purpose. Our task is to witness to the love of God as we understand it working in us.

I

Learning who we are is sometimes a painful endeavor. Persons who persist in sharp conflict with others are certainly trying to test knowledge of themselves against the world. If they succeed in learning about themselves through conflict, however, they will have to lick the wounds caused by angry words and suffer the embarrassment of disturbed communication. More often, though, the process of self-discovery takes place in a less conflicting and more creative fashion. This does not mean that creative self-understanding is free from struggle. Indeed, it is struggle in the finest sense if we let it take place within ourselves. If it takes place there we are spared the injury resulting from an unnecessary struggle with others. True, it is only the rare person that can discover himself without constant encounter with others. But the external encounter, to be valid, must be accompanied by the inner dialogue of "I think that . . . ," "I wonder whether . . . ," "It seems to me . . . ," "I suspect that. . . ." Such reflection about ourselves opens the way for God's spirit and will to enter the task of commitment and to govern the act of communication.

A good example of how this inner dialogue takes place can be found in the story of Jonah. "Now the word of the Lord came to Jonah . . . saying, 'Arise, and go to Nineveh.'" All we are told next is that Jonah immediately took off for Tarshish. A great deal must have happened inside Jonah between these two events. It is all left to our imagination, but from our understanding of human nature a few educated guesses can be made as to what went on. One can imagine the intrapersonal dialogue he carried on. He *wonders* how this will interrupt the familiar routine of his life; he *thinks* it will make an overpowering demand upon his personal resources; he *suspects* great personal risk; it *seems* that the whole idea is an attack upon his self-esteem. In fact, he was actually saying, "I do not trust myself enough to obey." It is little wonder that drastic action on God's part was necessary to lift Jonah to a higher level of self-understanding.

What Jonah experienced in this encounter with God is exactly what happens in our encounter with others. Every human contact arouses some perception of ourselves. When faced with unfamiliar people or situations, we may feel uneasy and unsure of ourselves. To others the same situation would mean challenge and adventure. The difference lies in the way we regard ourselves. The person whose inner struggle is limited to his own resources will become defensive and afraid in situations where the risk of failure is great, or where the reaction of others is unpredictable. But when the inner struggle is carried on within the will of God, risk can be tolerated since we are then able to rely on the resources of God's spirit.

To some extent everyone needs to protect his self-esteem, since the knowledge of ourselves is always incomplete. Life is therefore filled with self-protective devices we need to outgrow.

First, we can develop our life-style in a way that will avoid all threatening encounters. Indeed, one of our most serious temptations is to discover a familiar life path and follow it day after day. All our communication is with familiar people and situations. We may avoid contact with the kinds of persons who cause us to wonder, think, suspect, or reflect. Whenever serious discussion arises, we may become silent. If we face the power of individuals or groups whose habits or folkways we cannot understand, we retreat to the familiar with the feeling of disgust. Communication is neither tried nor wanted because we cannot see ourselves in such an unfamiliar situation.

Doubtless, no other behavior pattern stands in the way of creative living more than our attachment to the familiar. Groups and individuals with whom there is need for reconciliation or who can broaden our self-understanding are never encountered. Moving through a narrow world that does not challenge the inner notions about ourselves can result only in a divided community, each side of which intensifies its beliefs and enhances its own faulty perceptions of itself. Dialogue disappears, and when the goals of the communities are at serious enough variance, violence erupts.

Avoidance behavior restricts communication, which in turn makes commitment unnecessary. If there is no threat to the way we see ourselves, we have lost the need to carry on the inner dialogue from which commitment arises. Carrying it a step further, we have no need for God. In fact, if we are successful in protecting ourselves from attack, we may begin to mistake our self-perception for God. Instead of seeing God *in* ourselves, we see God *as* ourselves. There is no need for a God-man communication because the desire for commitment has vanished, and the experience of creative encounter has been avoided.

The second way to protect our self-image is to relate to others without ever expecting anything to change within ourselves. We are helped along in this faulty style of communication by two misconceptions: first, that personality is fully understood by classifying it; and second, that the Christian witness is the process of overcoming the beliefs (thoughts, ideas, commitments) of other people.

The restricted person divides mankind into *persons* (those who are acceptable to him) and *nonpersons* (those who are unacceptable). Buried somewhere in history is the story of how the word *person*, which originally meant a masking of the true self, came to refer to the inner nature and substance of the individual. In losing the "mask" meaning we may restrict the term *person* to a too-narrow concept. In Cicero's writings the word *person* suggests dignity and prestige, an individual with the qualities of courage, truth, and wisdom, fit to be a representative of his nation. As late as the nineteenth century the representative of the church was called a parson. Even today we apply the term *personages* to members of the "representative" class of people.

20

Although in theory we might apply the term *person* to the slave, the prisoner, the minority-group member, the outcast, and the poor, in reality we don't treat them as such because they are not "representative." That is, they do not represent the qualities of life we believe to be right and good. Their behavior disproves them.

All through history we have been educated to divide right from wrong as human behavior indicates it. In the Old Testament this classical concept is clearly set down. There is no Hebrew equivalent for the term *personality*. The inner form of man was the *nephesh* and the body was its outer form, so that what was happening in the outer form (body) was happening also in the inner form. Man was described by the quality of his behavior: he was a sluggard, worthless, evil, arrogant, and foolish, or he was wise, truthful, righteous, loyal, attentive, and prudent. Every individual was a particular type.

Later developments in Western culture refined the description of types of persons. The king was not the serf, the priest was not the people, the employer was not the employee, the teacher was not the pupil, the rich not the poor, the Protestant not the Catholic. Each was evaluated in his own special category. Add to this the fact that now people are also typed as to color, weight, height, intelligence, facial contour, and even skin thickness, the classification becomes complex. In other words, we all have to be something!

But the trouble arises when the "something" is restricted to the words and actions of the individual. We assume that what a man *does* is always what he *is*. But it would seem that the gospel tells us otherwise. It takes into account the fact that words and actions are only one aspect (and probably not the most important aspect) of personality. In addition, all persons commit themselves to action as a result of their intrapersonal communication. All people tend to mask

21

these feelings about themselves. In this, all people are alike. Whether king or serf, employer or employee, the dynamics of self-regard, commitment, and communication are exactly the same.

The one inescapable element in communication is the self. Other aspects of the individual's field appear, disappear, and reappear, but he remains in constant contact with his inner self. He is both actor and observer at the same time. For the communication theorist this poses some interesting problems. What is the nature of the self? Can intrapersonal communication achieve insight to correct man's internal life? The witness of the Christian faith is that man's communion with God is the primary source of creative action and self-appraisal. Man does not need to tell himself who he is. If he is truly Christian he accepts his internal environment as a gift of God, who is the "other person" involved in his intrapersonal communication. Instead of contemplating himself, his needs, frustrations, and inadequacies, he engages in a "bidding" discipline. He waits upon the Holy Spirit, and when the communication is established, he is opened to a changed and better-adapted internal environment, accompanied by a change in a conscious perception of his external environment.

II

Along with and related to some of our misconceptions about personality are the notions we hold about our witnessing tasks. That Christianity is a witnessing way of life is not open to doubt. Any religion that meets the needs of man must include his need for community and for communication. However, our faulty concept of personhood leads to an equally faulty concept of the way persons relate. Judging persons on the basis of behavior alone is perhaps the most convenient method of distinguishing those witnessing from those being witnessed to. This results in a simple and forthright attack upon the customs and life-style of persons outside the established community. It may become the struggle of one subculture against another sub-culture. And sometimes the conflict is not resolved by hon-est dialogue. We can only hope to win one at a time from "their number" to "our number." For example, to see the numerical strength of the church dwindling is to fear the advancement of the secular forces. We are only now begin-ning to see that witnessing is futile if confined to the tactic of persuading others to forsake one behavior pattern for another.

Witnessing is a form of commitment. It does not begin with words and gestures, but with the willingness to estab-lish community. This is an inner decision to sacrifice one's self in the interest of establishing the conditions under which the Holy Spirit can work his miracle of reconcilia-tion. In other words, we cannot pose as "witnesses" to the gospel. Rather, we are called upon to establish the kind of arena in which God's spirit "will convince the world of sin and of righteousness and of judgment" (John 16:8). And "the world" includes us. It is a mistake to set the Christian over against the world, to believe that the world must be brought to its knees because it is worldly. God speaks to and through all of us. The committed person who moves beyond the familiar setting of his worship and devotion is often surprised to find that God is already at work in those he is trying to reach. Community can be established only when we recognize his action in all humanity.

Witnessing is also a commitment to the possibility of change within ourselves. The fear of being won over to the other side makes us defend against changes and establishes one-way communication. The conversation is argumentative and persuasive. Threats of reprisal and punishment are used to defend against our uncertainties and need for growth and self-fulfillment. Aggressive and even judgmental speech serves only to frighten the weak and build up counteraggression in the strong. We blame our failures on *their* hardness of heart, *their* refusal to listen, and *their* love of waywardness. We cannot afford to listen because we cannot afford to change.

Late one night I was standing on an all but deserted railroad platform waiting for a train. It was cold and snowing. A man carrying a small bundle of papers came toward me and said, "I am interested in your soul. Are you saved?"

I thought of all the answers I could give, most of them being to defend my righteousness and to get rid of what could turn out to be a bothersome conversation. However, from somewhere deep inside me I felt the defenses melt away in favor of a desire to relate to him, and so I answered, "You must have deep convictions to come out on a cold night like this just to ask me that question."

He replied, "Well, I have a small church a couple blocks away and I need to do this. A woman in Tennessee sends me money to carry on this work. I think God wants me to do this."

"And you came to me to ask about my soul," I said.

"Yes, I do this with a lot of people. Some like it and some don't. I try to give them one of these papers I print and they usually take one. Who are you?"

"Well, like you, I'm a minister."

"Do you have a church?"

"No, I teach."

"Then you are different than me. I'm not educated. I just read my Bible and do what it says."

By this time I was getting caught up in the relationship. "I guess we are different. I'm supposed to be rather well educated and I imagine we would not agree on a lot of things."

The train was arriving and he seemed about to leave, so I said, "Aren't you going to give me one of your papers?"

"I don't think so. I make a lot of mistakes and I'm not too good with words." He hesitated for a moment, then said, "But I guess you wouldn't laugh at what I've done." He handed me a paper and left.

On the train I read parts of his paper and found that the distance between our concepts of the faith were so great that neither of us could have been convincing to the other. But for a brief time on that platform I felt a sense of community and of warmth at being in the presence of someone who had an interest in me. Who was witnessing to whom? This is immaterial. Of more importance is the fact that we were open to each other and therefore open to God's spirit.

To overcome our tendency to defend the faith by defending ourselves, our commitment must be to the whole man and to the development of community. All too often we try to cover up the fact that we are searching. Even the most rigid and dogmatic person is, at the center of his life, searching for "salvation"—a secure position from which he can be productive and useful. Not being willing to risk a commitment to community, he bombards his environment with ideas and structures. These are weak and ineffective substitutes for the feeling of community. Ideas and concepts alone cannot establish community. Our professions of faith and agreements on worship forms may only serve to draw together persons who feel safe in each other's presence because they see eye-to-eye or "mind-to-mind." Worship then becomes an exercise in reinforcement instead of an expression of community.

There is no effective communication without community, and no complete understanding of community without reference to the love of God. God always acts in our behalf. His grace to us is his concern for the whole person. Until

25

we feel and know that we are loved, we cannot expect to communicate that love. To participate in expressions of love is the goal of all persons. To be a witness to that love is the responsibility of all Christians. In this process, change can take place in ourselves as well as in others.

Perception of the world, of persons, and of who we are in relation to them is a hidden activity. Others may know we are pondering, wondering, and calculating, but they can only guess what is going on inside. Our intrapersonal communication is private and self-regulated. Sooner or later, however, it will have to be expressed. Our inner lives motivate us into action. Others want us to express ourselves. "A penny for your thoughts" is a direct invitation to test ourselves in the presence of another. Sometimes the pressure of the inner self is so great that we "just had to say something" or "just had to get it off our chest." At other times our perception of the situation is so threatening that wild horses could not get us to express ourselves. But the suppression can only be temporary. In one way or another, the act of communicating within ourselves will find its way into our relations with others.

It is at this point that the term *communication* is generally used and understood. When we move from *intra*personal to *inter*personal activity, our lives are made public and we reveal something of ourselves. No matter how hard we try to express ourselves secretly or to use codes we think others will not understand, there is always the logical possibility that our code can be broken and our secret revealed. Talk will be heard and motion will be seen or felt. Therefore, the moment we perform the activity of conversation, discussion, preaching, teaching, or entertaining, we have become responsible to those engaged with us. We are in the public domain where our actions are observed and evaluated. When a person says or does something inappropriate or damaging to others, he must go through a lot of explaining and search for forgiveness. Even then the embarrassment lingers on and may never be forgotten. He wishes he hadn't said it and that he could take it all back.

All words and gestures have meaning, but meaning is not to be found in the words and gestures themselves. Of course, there is consensus on a great many forms of human expression. Otherwise, it would be impossible to communicate. Society seems to press toward uniformity in the use of language and gesture so that objects and even concepts can readily be identified. However, meanings universally given to objects are nearly always accompanied by the personal meaning the individual has given to the object. Take spinach, for instance. I suppose nearly everyone would agree it's a green, leafy vegetable, but beyond this many persons would attach private meanings to it. They like it or they don't. They might be reminded of parental authority or associate it with a remembered event in their lives. If one happens to be a horticulturist, it isn't a vegetable at all but a potherb of the goosefoot family. Language, as Lee says,

> is not a system of names for passively sensed objects and relations already existing in the outer world; but neither does it fit experience into predetermined molds. It is a creative process in which the individual has an agentive function; it is part of a field which contains, in addition, the world of physical reality, the sensing and thinking individual, and the experienced reality. In this way each word, each grammatical formation, is not an empty label to be applied; it has meaning, not because meaning has been arbitrarily assigned to it, but because it contains the meaning of the concrete situation in which it participates and has participated, and which it has helped create.[1]

By nature, man makes a value judgment in what he thinks and feels. His responses arise from the commitments

1. D. Lee, "Symbolization and Value," in Lyman Bryson, ed., *Symbols and Values: An Initial Study* (New York: Harper & Row, 1954), p. 73.

in his inner self, and his words and gestures are symbolic representations of this inner self. He is able to escape the confines of the natural world. He gives a spiritual meaning to things, even if he has to create one for himself. Cassirer recognizes this:

> Man cannot escape from his own achievement. He cannot but adopt the conditions of his own life. No longer in a merely physical universe, man lives in a symbolic universe. Language, myth, art, and religion are parts of this universe. They are the varied threads which weave the symbolic net, the tangled web of human experience. All human progress in thought and experience refines upon and strengthens this net. No longer can man confront reality immediately; he cannot see it, as it were, face to face. Physical reality seems to recede in proportion as man's symbolic activity advances. Instead of dealing with the things themselves man is in sense constantly conversing with himself. He has so enveloped himself in linguistic forms, in artistic images, in mythical symbols or religious rites that he cannot see or know anything except by the interposition of this artificial medium. His situation is the same in the theoretical as in the practical sphere. Even here man does not live in a world of hard facts, or according to his immediate needs and desires. He lives rather in the midst of imaginary emotions, in hopes and fears, in illusions and disillusions, in his fantasies and dreams. "What disturbs and alarms man," said Epictetus, "are not the things, but his opinions and fancies about the things."[2]

It is exactly at this point that religious education and therapy face their task. From the deep inner life of one person to the inner life of another, communication is deeper than its symbols and gestures. It must therefore be relevant to the source from which the symbols are derived. For the Christian, the source is the love of God and the establishment of the community of God's people.

2. Ernst Cassirer, *An Essay on Man* (New Haven: Yale University Press, 1944), p. 25.

Knowing that communication requires us to act at the level of our deep commitments, joys, sorrows, doubts, fears, and ambitions, we are always faced with the question of how much of ourselves we are going to reveal. There is a prevailing tendency to encourage people to unmask themselves, to express their feelings, and otherwise to drop their defenses and bare their souls. One cannot dispute the fact that the community is strengthened in direct relation to the quality and depth of human sharing. However, love demands responsible and appropriate action. This may require assertive and free expression, or it may call for some withholding. Always, however, we must be appropriate. Of all the possible means of expression in any given situation, there is one that will show the most love and make the greatest contribution to the life of the community. Of course, it is neither easy nor possible to express love perfectly and appropriately in every situation. We soon learn that the skill of "finding" others is as difficult to attain as is the skill of "finding" God.

The unloving person has little trouble expressing himself. He moves into all situations without reference to the situation itself. His fears and resentments obscure his true self. He does not seek change toward an improved community; he seeks change only in the other person. The loving person is sensitive and authentic. He searches for the type of change that will lift everyone, including himself, to a higher level of community life.

First, commitment to God and man requires us to be sensitive to the shifts and changes in the demands made upon us by our world. We live in a multitude of fields, and even those most familiar to us do not remain constant. Each situation has its unique need for something unique from us. Earlier we referred to the solidarity and unity of community in the Old Testament. Within this unity, communication could be forthright, open, and honest. In a pluralistic society such as ours, communication is more tentative, devious, and protective. An example of this can be found in the wars between the Israelites and the Philistines (1 Samuel 4:12–18). The Philistines had won an overwhelming victory. A runner came from the battlefield to Shiloh where Eli, the aged and blind prophet, was waiting for news. The runner came right up to the old man and blurted out the news that Eli's two sons had been killed, the battle lost, and the ark of God captured. Eli fell off his seat, broke his neck, and died. Under the conditions prevailing in their community, there was nothing irregular about proceeding in this way. Under present conditions, concern for persons would make the delivery of this message somewhat more tentative and cautious. How can we tell the old man? Who is the best person to tell him? How can we prevent him from falling off his chair and breaking his neck? Elsewhere[3] I have discussed the "bidding" approach to the environment. Waiting upon God for the assessment and inspiration of our inner life is not unlike the process of evaluating the environment to determine how it will stimulate us into action. God is in the world just as he is in us. We must learn how to listen to it.

Second, appropriate expression means that we should be authentic. Effective communication requires us to fit in according to the role we play in the situation. Here we run into a current problem of self-expression. People are heard to say they don't want to play a role, they just want to be themselves. Like all other concepts of personality, the role concept can easily be abused. The clergyman can hide behind his profession, the teacher behind his authority, the Protestant behind his dogma. If this happens, communication will not originate from our commitment to God and persons, but from our commitment to the role we play.

3. Harry DeWire, *The Christian as Communicator* (Philadelphia: Westminster Press, 1960).

Moreover, others soon come to evaluate the strength of that role and submit to it. "If the minister said it, it must be true." "Why should I obey? Because he is an adult and I am a child."

People are being fooled less and less by the power of social roles. The counterculture being shaped by youth has made this a major issue. They protest against the "Establishment," against teachers, and against all people who use their roles as a substitute for the authentic person. However, the fault lies not so much in the concept of role as it does in the use we make of our roles. Whether we like it or not, we must occupy concrete social positions simply to be able to function. Being a parent, employer, teacher, or minister automatically establishes a unique relationship with a child, employee, pupil, or parishioner. One study[4] has shown that during a normal lifetime, one person must learn to master approximately twenty-five roles, each of which stands in contrast to an opposite role played by another person.

Our roles are signs, or designations of social position and function. They tell us *where we are* but not *who we are*. We bring to others not only what is socially designated, but more important, what is personally authentic. Let's look at an example of how these roles get in our way and what can be done about it. Suppose you want to visit a friend or a member of your parish in the hospital. The roles are already established: you are well and your friend is ill. You wonder how to communicate with a sick person. Show sympathy? Treat him like a helpless person? Shower him with flowers, candy, and other evidences that you are in the favored position? You can do any number of things that will only emphasize the fact that you are not interested in the person as a person, but as a sick someone. In addi-

4. Jurgen Ruesch and Gregory Bateson, *Communication: The Social Matrix of Psychiatry* (New York: W. W. Norton, 1951).

tion, you may find it hard to resist being glad you are where you are (well) and he is where he is (ill). J. H. van den Berg makes some suggestions as to how this role difference can be handled.

> In general, it is not advisable to prepare oneself for a visit to a patient. The chances are that the prepared conversation will prevail over the topics the patient really wants to discuss, so that, although he may be taking part in a lively conversation, he is never given a chance to say what he wants to say. One thing should be kept in mind though; the visitor should always realize that the human threshold he crosses is higher than the one at the door of the sickroom. He should also be aware of the fact that exact height of the threshold will be unknown to him until the words of the patient have made its measurement clear. Abandoning our metaphor, the visitor should try to find the patient in the latter's own world and discuss there the subjects that are significant in his exceptional existence. He should put himself in the place of the patient and since the patient can only permit this if he is permitted in his turn to put himself in the place of the visitor, the latter should talk about his problems exactly as he would if he were visiting a healthy acquaintance. In a word, the visitor acts normally.[5]

Our true role in all situations is to act in such a manner that all elements—our own nature, the meaning of the other person, the will of God, and the demands of the situation itself—are evaluated and dealt with appropriately. Actually, this is another way of saying that this is the way the loving person communicates. He loves because he can be true and faithful to all the nuances and requirements of an interpersonal event. This is the only way to master our roles. We will always be recognized as teachers, clergymen, or parents, but we will be remembered as persons who knew how to express themselves appropriately.

5. J.H. van den Berg, *The Psychology of the Sickbed* (Pittsburgh: Duquesne University Press, 1966), pp. 78–79.

In the third place, the loving person will want to express himself in such a way that the resulting change will promote growth. All communication brings change, and all spiritual exercise and endeavor are designed to bring about change. Change is not necessarily growth, and communication is often disturbed simply because the participants in the process either do not understand or are not willing to tolerate the kind of change being sought. Some want to change others to be like themselves. Others want change only if it does not disturb the sources of comfort they enjoy. Still others look for the kind of change that will bring all people into conformity with prevailing group norms. We may justify such change only on the basis of a narrow perception of ourselves, the will of God, and other people.

"Love seeks not its own." Rather, it seeks the improvement of all elements in the situation. This includes and demands growth in communication. Entering an interpersonal event with the expectation that we will be changed for the better may be the hardest thing we do. Moreover, as we have seen there is no true community unless all its members are educated, judged, and guided by the Holy Spirit. Even when we express ourselves with certainty, we are especially under the ministry of God's spirit, for no matter how accurately we have judged what needs to be said and done, God's ways are not always ours.

Communication that builds people into a growing community develops certain skills of its own. Love has a language. It is learned mostly by trial and error, but gets most of its direction from the spirit we bring to the situation. Happy persons usually say and do happy things, but even then, what is said might not meet the needs of persons around us. If we become irate, we are still faced with the problem of knowing what to say that will meet the demands both within ourselves and within others. In our culture, interpersonal relationships as well as social structures are initiated and dissolved frequently. We move quickly from one encounter to another. People attending a committee meeting may be called by their first names and then not hear from each other in months.

Is there a single communication skill that will fit into all situations? Is there a peculiar stance that can be taken by the Christian that will assure the growth of persons and community in all situations? It might be thought that to search for such consistency would violate the principle of appropriateness. This is true enough if the only communication skills we learn are to speak and gesture. Of course these will vary. But how about the skill of listening? This aspect of communication is constant. To learn to listen is to learn the one skill that applies equally to all situations. This will be looked at in more detail in the next chapter.

Chapter III

LISTENING

Human expression takes many forms. There are many ways to move intrapersonal dialogue into interpersonal encounter. Much of the time we must act quickly, responding before thinking. To gain control of the situation we use words and gestures freely. When we speak of communication, we are usually thinking of the process of word and gesture exchange. In doing so, we may miss the point of communication altogether. Speech and action are the symbols of the process, not the process itself. The meanings behind the expression are not the true substance of communication; nor are meaning and expression put together, no matter how clearly our gestures and words express our meanings.

Human community is developed neither by the clarity with which we express ourselves nor by the degree to which we are honest with each other. Even if we are both clear and honest, there is no guarantee that we will relate to others effectively. In fact, honesty may hurt, and clarity (on our part) may deprive the other person of the privilege of searching. At best, all outward human expression is designed and used to control, to shape the environment, and to provide the raw material out of which communication grows. Such expression meets the need to make contact with our companions, to inform and state facts, to create, to protest, and to assert our existence. But at the same time, words and actions are the chief causes of disturbed communication. They can hypnotize, seduce, flatter, confuse, slander, and condemn. Even our silence (withholding expression) may be a symbol of hostility.

Where do we find the one factor that can move us through our intrapersonal commitment to our commitment to the world while maintaining our search for the will of God? It must certainly be some sort of physical expression, for human nature is set to act. It must also be creative and perform all the positive functions performed by words and gestures. At the same time, it must be free from all disturbing influences that other forms of communication can cause. Only one human function can accomplish this: the art and spirit of listening. A surprising number of works on communication make little or no reference to listening, and when they do, it is usually to describe the ability to be attentive to and perceptive of others in their relationships. Obviously, this is an important part of listening, but by no means all there is to it.

Listening is a way of life. It is the stance we take in the process of intrapersonal communication. We listen for God, for understanding of our capabilities, for the knowledge of what is expected of us. We listen to ourselves expressing our thoughts and feelings in words and actions; we listen to the reaction to our expression and to the responses made to them. Furthermore, listening is itself an expression that can be felt by others in our interpersonal relationships. More than a gesture of politeness or a convenient way of dividing conversation equally, it is the character or mode of the person's participation in life.

I

To listen is to respond. This occurs not only during our periods of silence but in the words we speak. In fact, communication is a combination of two forms of commitment —a commitment to certainty and a commitment to openness. Both of these must take place simultaneously. All speech can be listening-oriented if we speak so as to demonstrate our certainty by a willingness to continue to search for God's spirit and will and for the meanings beneath the expressions of others. To be open is to maintain contact with the source of our commitment and to keep alive the spirit of love upon which the establishment of community depends. God is as much with us in our search as he is in our certainty. Rigidity (certainty without search) is the denial of God's movement in our acts of communication. This is what Paul must have meant when he said, "If I have prophetic powers, and understand all mysteries and all knowledge, and if I have all faith so as to remove mountains, but have not love, I am nothing" (1 Corinthians 13:2). I am nothing to other persons. I am nothing in my own search for the love of God.

The word *nothing* deserves looking at. Using it as Paul does leads us to suppose that the person without love is out of the picture. Were this the case, communication generally would cause some improvement. But on the contrary, such a person is very much in the picture—along with a broad array of his defenses. Communication is disturbed by his repression, denial, projection, and rationalization. These require so much energy that his hearer has neither the time nor the disposition to listen. Moreover, such defensiveness is prejudiced behavior. Certainty has taken over completely at the expense of openness and love. Paul suggests that our knowledge, understanding, and faith enough to remove mountains are nothing without love. The biased person sees others as mountains to be moved, as having beliefs to be overcome. Along the way the biased person has developed effective means of employing certainty without listening.

First, he is equipped with an overabundance of "hard" speech. This is speech designed to maintain categorical structures in keeping with his defenses. All words are potent, but some are more potent than others. For instance, suppose we refer to someone as a "popular fundamentalist preacher." Each of these words is potent, but in religious circles the word *fundamentalist* would undoubtedly be the most potent of the three. It becomes even more potent when used by itself to describe someone: "He is a fundamentalist." Religious language is laced with a surprising number of "hard" words and phrases—atheist, liberal, radical, the name of almost any denomination, backslider, agnostic, bigot, unbeliever, noncommunicant member, noncontributing member, pious, hard-shell, hypocrite, modernist, to name just a few. It is inevitable that we use words to classify persons: there are entirely too many people in the world to deal with individually or as a total group. But the categories of people provide the prejudiced person with a sounding board against which he can justify his defenses. He is defending his Bible, his faith, his religion, his God, and his creed against the people of the categories he opposes.

Second, the prejudiced person refuses to listen for fear that others might press him to examine what he is saying. The communication process is closed once he has expressed himself. No feedback is permitted, and the communicator has thus denied himself and others the correctives necessary to find their way into a genuine community. He does not even listen to himself. Also, in his desire to be certain, the true quest for certainty is frustrated. If we agree that the entire process of communication is characterized by listening, then the point at which listening stops is the point at which information, insight, and enlightenment stop. The kind of speech used to cut off the listening process is all too familiar to us. We may say, "I can't help it, that's the way I see it," "I've made up my mind," or "I don't want to discuss it any further." The other person in the relationship becomes the "enemy" against whom we have to defend. There must be an answer to every question. We cannot admit that we don't know, and so our strong defense might well have put the other person on the defensive. This is the breakdown of communication, the "nothing" about which Paul speaks.

II

Foremost among the requirements for Christian commitment is the recognition that regardless of the strength of our commitment, we remain persons of great need, and we communicate with persons and within situations of great need. These needs can be understood and dealt with only if we keep ourselves open and sensitive to the nuances of our personal involvement in human encounter.

Our needs are always with us, even though we have been taught to show how strong and self-reliant we are. To need is to be dependent and even submissive to others, but all too often we act as though our Christian faith cannot thrive on such a display of weakness. Nevertheless, the list of our needs expands. We need intimacy, physical satisfactions, acceptance, the opportunity to serve and help, to instruct and to learn, to exercise power, to "keep up with things," to enter conflict, and to create. None of these needs can be met apart from the communication process. Whether the process be intrapersonal or interpersonal, the act of prayer or conversation, preaching or worshiping, we come to the situation with a void to be filled. Both other persons and God can meet these needs, but not while we maintain our defenses against them. Listening is the art of putting ourselves into the hands of both God and others, for they are the primary resources for meeting our need.

Usually we do not have much difficulty with the suggestion that we put ourselves into the hands of God and listen for ways he can meet our needs. This is the basic status of man before God. We view our commitment to God as a search for answers to our quandaries, for improved understanding of some element of faith, or for a decision toward more effective behavior. To be sure, our commitment to God is not always open and receptive. Again, voicing our prayers often is a commitment to certainty at the expense of openness, and we suppose that God's will must fall somewhere within the boundaries of the things we ask for. But, of course, he may have other things in mind for us. What we need and what God thinks we need might not be identical.

So the art of listening should begin with, or at least be reinforced by, the way we act in our solitude. To listen in the presence of God is to know and not to know, to ask and not to ask, to find and not to find. We may be too easily influenced by the simple and direct admonition, "Seek and ye shall find. . . ." This is not a simple matter of cause and effect, where we tell God what we want or need and then expect an answer. Nor does it help much to give God some leeway by permitting him to answer our prayers in ways not consistent with our requests. In other words, there isn't much good in telling God that if we can't have our way it's all right for him to have things his way.

There are many ways to act in the presence of God: talk to him, bargain with him, engage in something called dialogue with him. As valid as these are as ways of finding what we are searching for, they fall short of listening to God. If our attention is on the *finding,* we are apt to miss the strength and value of the *seeking*. In fact, to seek is the only action open to us. When we say, "Lord, thou art here," our next utterance should be, "'But Lord, where art thou?'" If we ask of God, we should be sensitive to the fact that there is a futility in our asking, since our waywardness makes us very poor beggars. To say that we have found is to recognize that we have found only in part and that what we have found may eventually need to be changed and improved upon. It is the constant search that keeps us within the love and will of God. The certainty of his love and will are valueless without our being open to the search for his love and will.

Listening to God creates a strong demand upon our lives. This can take the form of a specific commitment, an improved understanding of our faith, or a decision to take more effective action in the world. This demand is a commitment, a call to witness to what we have learned and felt. Being dominated by both certainty and commitment, we are now ready to communicate. At this crucial moment, when we move from hearing God's message to performing God's mission, a subtle change may take place. Although we may permit ourselves to be receptive and even submissive in the presence of God, we may feel strong and dominant in the presence of man. To proclaim this message we take advantage of the most obvious and accessible forms of human expression: speech and gesture. For many people the word *message* connotes some form of speech.

There can be no doubt that there is a message. Without it we leave ourselves open to the question as to whether the Christian cannot be certain, positive, or straightforward about anything. Are there no absolutes? Have not the test of time, the witness of the saints, and the experience of the church taught us that we should not be trumpets giving uncertain sounds? Exactly so, but it is God's message, not ours, and we must commit it to the world.

Although it is his message, it is our mission in spite of our incompleteness. Our needs are *not* fully met once we have finished communing with God. If nothing else, the need for fellowship and community are still present. We need to test what we have heard from our *intra*personal communication within the *inter*personal dialogue. It can be tested only if we are as open to man as we have been open to God. The process in committing ourselves to man is exactly the same as it is in committing ourselves to God. We are both certain and open. We listen, even in our proclaiming. In talking to another we are inviting God to meet *our* needs in exactly the way he met *my* needs.

III

The recognition that need exists is only one reason why it is important to develop the art of listening. A second and equally important reason grows out of man's capacity to live in anticipation of a more gratifying life. We constantly harbor the hope that our lives will be more fulfilled as the result of our experiences. The Christian faith has always encouraged us to anticipate a better world, a sinless afterlife, and a more favorable position for those who do God's will. For many, hope lies in the expectation that God will intervene in the scheme of things to meet our needs. Others set out to fulfill their needs and the needs of the world by becoming engaged in causes and movements. Still others seek out a therapeutic relationship to learn about themselves, hoping to find more satisfying ways to cope with life.

It is easy to mistake hope for an optimistic outlook on life. The oppressed want a better life in the hereafter; the ill, a cure. The social actionist believes the cause he represents will improve the structure and function of society. Some persons entertain the hope that time will make others see their "truths" the way they do. This kind of optimism produces support for the ego and arises out of a set notion of how things should be.

Our difficulties with hope grow out of our particular type of orientation to the past and present. For many, God's revelation in the life and work of the church is the last word. Any view of the future must be cast in forms and terms already known, if not fully understood. Yet the fact that much in the past is still unexplained makes us wistful. How can we look to the future with so much of the past yet to be known? We are naive about theological systems. While we develop a "feeling tone" about the Christian community and learn to make appropriate responses to its demands, we cannot always anchor our behavior to satisfying systems of belief.

Furthermore, we always stand some distance away from the primary sources of our faith. The origin of the Christian message often remains anonymous. Even listening to a sermon we are reminded that the minister does not speak without reference to things written or said by other people, who in turn have read or heard what has been said and written by still others. We are awed by the firsthand experiences of Moses, Saul of Tarsus, Joan of Arc, and Bernadette of Lourdes. We wonder how it happened or even whether it happened. More to the point, because we do not expect it to happen to us, we regard these experiences of the past as normative for our belief but not for our own lives.

Our preoccupation with the past has been reinforced by the techniques used to help people deal with their troubles. Psychoanalysis has held out the promise that by understanding the events of our past, we can somehow cope with the future. A student working as a counselor in a county prison was about to interview a prisoner for the first time. The prisoner started the conversation by saying, "Do you want to hear about my mother?" More recently psychotherapy has opened more realistic approaches through existential (the discovery of meaning and acceptance of responsibility) and phenomenological (taking the person's own view of himself as a unique being-in-the-world) processes. While these are good starting points for self-discovery, they lack the note of destiny, of hope beyond the present. Sometimes it seems we have not moved far from Sartre's preoccupation with the despair, dread, and anguish from which there is "no exit" and to which we can only respond by keeping a stiff upper lip.

With an obscure past, an unacceptable present, and an uncertain future it is little wonder that a sizable number of persons turn to religious groups that promise superhuman deliverance or to causes that require action. This is not to say that those who search for answers to life are without hope. In many cases, quite the contrary. The difference lies in what the action anticipates. Hope is an emotion directed toward redemption and reconciliation. Like faith and love, it is the way we encounter and cope with any situation. It is the commitment to community.

If communication is the medium by which we commit our lives to one another, it must take on only those characteristics that draw persons together. This is the Christian message *and* mission, the certainty *and* the openness. Both are caught up in the single act of communication. It is not enough to talk about reconciliation, to point to the evidences of it in the past, or even to point to its coming at some future time. We are called to *be* "reconciliation," to hope for the presence of God's healing power in every human dialogue.

In the process of communication, hope and listening are inseparable. Paul Pruyser makes an interesting distinction between "embeddedness affect" and "activity affect."[1] He

1. Paul W. Pruyser, *A Dynamic Psychology of Religion* (New York: Harper & Row, 1968), pp. 164 ff.

44

sees the first as a feeling of helpless distress, an escape from the reality by wishing something to happen. In this case the self is important. To listen would destroy what has been embedded, which is seen to be ultimate truth. It would destroy the feeling that the God we have heard is our private possession, and that he has not been at work in other places.

"Activity affect" is the emotion that stimulates the person to goal-directed action and reaches out for the reality of the others even at the expense of self-enhancement. The person puts himself on the line, so to speak. He is convinced there is a possibility of creating novelty that transcends what he knows from the past and the present. Hope causes him to listen. It is the only posture of anticipation available to human life. Hope is the affect; listening is the style of life. We have only a limited knowledge of things that can be. The certainty of one God, one creation, and one salvation does not close off the way the oneness expresses itself. As Phillips Brooks tells it in "O Little Town of Bethlehem":

How silently, how silently the wondrous gift is given;
So God imparts to human hearts the blessings of his heaven.
No ear may hear his coming, but in this world of sin
Where meek souls will receive him still,
The dear Christ enters in.

IV

Earlier it was suggested that listening is a form of response, an active style of life in the communication process. It must go even further to be a full commitment. It needs to affirm, to witness, to proclaim. This sounds like a lot to ask of a behavior pattern usually associated with passivity and even weakness. But how often we are told what seems weak to us may indeed be God's strength, that what seems foolish may indeed be wise. It is time to see that the listening mood is the strong ingredient that moves our commitment into a community of love. This affirmation takes place in at least four ways.

1. *Listening affirms the self.* It is easy to equate self with energy, action, and even aggression. The person who exhibits the qualities of persuasion and can take command of a situation is, in the minds of many, a person who certainly must have a high self-esteem. Total commitment is usually interpreted to mean exactly the opposite of self-affirmation. To be committed is thought to be synonymous with self-forgetting, self-sacrificing, self-denying, self-giving, and even self-effacing. Throughout their history Christians have symbolized this kind of commitment by inflicting all sorts of punishment upon themselves. Both body and mind have been denied their delights and joys in the interest of being "offered" sacrificially. But listening provides us with the most viable means of evaluating ourselves in the communication process. It is a means of providing feedback from ourselves. Are we free to feel the joy of being a person? How much anxiety and doubt about our own concepts are we bringing to the encounter? Can we view accurately the alternation between certainty and openness in our own lives? Where are the points at which we are immune to our surroundings? Communication is always disturbed when we "turn ourselves loose" without listening to what we are saying.

Some early unusual experiences with my grandfather taught me a lot about the way we listen to ourselves. He was a retired railroader and was never without a large pocket watch. Asked what time it was, he would set in motion a ritual so interesting that sometimes I would want to know the time of day even when I didn't care. First he would come to the posture of attention. If he were walking, he would stop. I never saw him tell anyone the time while he was in motion. While reaching for his watch he would look at the person who asked him, probably to find out whether he had heard correctly. Watch in hand, he ran his thumb over the glass face and said something like, "The time, huh?" By this time I would get the impression he was making my question his own. He liked to watch himself in the process. He was rather proud of his watch, his ability to tell time, and his railroader's experience in reading what the watch indicated. His answer always started out, "Well, according to my watch . . . ," and he always gave the time to the half minute. All through this process, I got the impression he had a high level of self-esteem in this integrated function of his personality.

Listening to ourselves in our encounter with the world is only one step away from communication with the source of power and love. This might be the most difficult step, since our relation to God requires fewer defenses than our encounter with man. But at the same time, if we can carry over the process of listening in which we are affirmed in the presence of God, we will find similar affirmation if we listen to ourselves in conversation with the world.

2. *Listening helps us affirm not only who we are but where we are.* Communication always occurs in context. Not only do we always have to be somewhere. Where we are must always make a difference in "how" we are. The person who takes pride in his consistency of behavior at all times and places is only revealing his unwillingness to listen and to accept the "'gift-of-this-place" he has been given. The unbending Protestant who finds himself in a Roman Catholic sanctuary might find it difficult to give thanks for being there. The person whose motion is voted down might well wish he had not come to the meeting.

Much of the time we can make the decision about where we are going to be. Usually we will search out the familiar, the nonthreatening situation in which our refusal to listen is not challenged. Sometimes we have no choice, and we find ourselves where we don't want to be. To be stricken with serious illness leaves us with no choice about the reality of our being. Sometimes it is not ourselves, but our environment that changes around us. The world is full of long hair, strange ideas, odd changes from what we knew to be "where we were." The person who cannot be open to these shifts in his context of living can never find it possible to give God thanks for them and affirm his own presence in them. Such stresses on our normal way of life hardly ever create new problems; they simply sharpen the old ones. If we have functioned with an "embedded affect," or helpless rigidity, our immediate reaction will be to refuse to be grateful or to accept what is given. In such a situation we do not really exist, since we cannot participate in it. Communication then is not commitment to reconciliation, but a struggle to determine who wins the battle.

Only by listening can we affirm the reality of our being-in-the-world. Are we in God's house? In the street? About our work? Alone? Our surroundings are ever new and challenging. If they have become boring to us, that boredom may be traced to our refusal to tune our senses to the task of affirming the gift of our environment. To be sure, the given is always contaminated by our activity, but God works within our affairs to provide us with novel and unexpected disclosures of himself.

We must learn to listen for overtones and undertones, to read between the lines, to accept the circumstances of our existence. Victor Frankl spent several years in a concentration camp. His book *From Death Camp to Existentialism*[2] describes the discovery he made when his life was reduced to the sheer necessity for survival. When he found that nothing else had meaning, there was still the basic freedom to choose the attitude he would take toward his fate. This did not change the environment, but it greatly

2. Translated by Ilse Lasch (Boston: Beacon Press, 1959).

changed the person. We cannot carry through our commitment if we do not learn, as did Paul, "in whatever state I am, to be content."

To listen and to accept the reality of our encounter with the world provides a vital bridge between intrapersonal and interpersonal communication. It is the matter of getting our bearings in the transition from "I" to "thou," to know both who I am and where I am. What part do I play? Do I take the initiative or wait for someone else to take it? Is it a situation from which I can receive more than I can give? A host of questions must be answered before we begin to express ourselves. This is the process of establishing community, a commonness necessary for communication. Even when the situation suggests conflict, the committed person instinctively looks for the common ground. If nothing else this can be found in the fact that we are in the presence of persons like ourselves. Regardless of how we may differ, the human characteristics we share in common outnumber the differences.

3. *Listening affirms the presence and integrity of the other.* To some extent, every interpersonal encounter begins with some degree of "immunity," even with the acceptance of some sense of community. Perhaps this is why we have adopted "How are you?" as a popular form of greeting. The immunity is probably mutual. Communication serves to move us from one level of community to another, but no matter how well people know each other, each meeting should take place in a spirit of both need and hope. We recognize the fact that no person is without the need to grow; likewise, no relationship between persons is without the need to develop. By listening we recognize and accept the distance between ourselves and the other person.

Moreover, this immunity helps us to listen to the other one who, to some extent, feels alien to us. We respect the fact that no matter how common our cause, no matter how cooperative our actions, we remain unique and equally subject to the will of God. The day of Pentecost found the followers of Jesus gathered in one place. Their common grief, awe, and searching drew them toward each other. But when the spirit of God came, it did not light a fire in their midst. It descended upon the heads of each one. The message was privately given and privately received. In all relationships a person might well say, "We are one—but I am one, and the other person is one." What God has shown me may be the same as what he has shown others, but the process of being shown is and always will be a private process, no matter how strong the bonds that join us.

One of the most obvious ways this principle is violated can be found in some group discussions. When someone makes a statement or suggestion, another person will easily say, "That's what I said awhile ago," or "That's what I meant." The implication is that someone is stealing my stuff. This is apt to be especially irritating if the group acts on the suggestion of the other person rather than on ours. Or an unproductive argument starts, with such conflict of opinion, and the communication process turns into a struggle to see whose opinions will survive.

In neither of these cases is affirmation of the person taking place. We need to be agreed with, to be supported, and to secure affirmation of ourselves by others. We cannot listen because we want to be listened to. We are telling the other person we cannot or will not affirm him or grant him the right to be the recipient of God's will. It is little wonder that many persons can respond only with hostility. And it is hard to believe that people really listen; even when they do, it is often polite silence.

There is almost no easy way to disagree with people or even to show them "in love" where they are wrong. So why try? The correction of error is always a mutual endeavor.

When conflict arises, the listening person will say, "We disagree on this; let's push both our ideas along a little further until we find a solution." This might be called *volitional communication,* in which each person is acting on his own terms without being overpowered by the other. If one person comes to realize he *is* wrong, he still knows he is free to say so because he decides, and not because he is disagreed with.

To affirm the right of the other person is to love, and the fulfillment of the commandment "You shall love your neighbor as yourself." This is sometimes interpreted to mean that we love others in the same way we regard ourselves. Such an interpretation would lead us too easily to listen only as a means of affirming ourselves. We are much closer to the meaning of the commandment if we love others who have been created in exactly the same way we have been created. We give them the right to affirm themselves in our presence. The art of listening is the expression of ultimate concern—not *about* the behavior of the person, but *for* the person.

4. *To listen is to affirm the act of reconciliation.* In all his creative and sustaining power, God has been "mindful" of man. God visits us and supremely strives to bring us to him. He wants to make us whole by entering our lives. But he accomplishes this by invitation, not by force. Jesus' movement among men was seen by the early church as a series of acts aimed at the joining of broken parts and people. The words are healing words—touch, bind, come, arise, forgive, "go your way," "sin no more," walk. These words were natural to him because it was natural for him to act in a reconciling way.

It is impossible to learn to be reconciling without learning to listen as indicated in the three previous steps. By choosing this way of dealing with ourselves, our environ-

51

ment, and other persons we are *learning* to learn to act redemptively. Sometimes this is called the process of "deuterolearning." From the context of listening (the commitment to be reconciling) we learn to be reconciling. But only by wanting to be a reconciling person can we learn to be one. In each of the previous steps we have a viable setting for learning to communicate as a Christian.

The discipline of listening requires both patience and persistence. Our society generally encourages us to be quick and diffuse in our actions. We don't stay with one thing very long. Industry wants us to be quick. We are stimulated by so many and varied sights and sounds that our interest spans have been shortened. All this makes the task of "centering down" within the lives of others extremely difficult. But only by our commitment to communication which invites another into a search for community can the gospel of love be expressed.

Chapter IV

LANGUAGE

Once we have committed ourselves to the search for community and have developed a style of listening that permits that search to take place, *how* do we do things? What should take place in the overt acts of communication? From the scientist's point of view, the processes of forming sounds, speaking, and hearing are governed by principles that are now generally recognized. All human societies have languages, and in each of these societies language performs a similar function. It is basic to human conduct and survival, permits the person to establish his place in the community, and provides a means for introducing the young and the outsider into the norms and objectives of group life.

The scientist also pays attention to the more subtle forms of language—gesture, facial expression, mode of walk, dress, etiquette, way emotion is displayed, and manner in which people celebrate. What an impressive collection of skills man has to carry on transactions with the world around him. Where verbal language is neither possible nor appropriate we immediately begin to gesture or move our mouths as though we were talking. A glance can establish a common bond. Touch can convey a host of meanings.

But the scientist gets into deeper and more troublesome water when he tries to explain the dynamic relationship brought about by word and gesture. All we do and say is the direct result of some form of inner commitment. "By their fruits you shall know them" is never taken quite literally. It is not difficult to observe and interpret the expressive acts of those around us, but the nature of the commitment behind them often remains a mystery. Is the overattentive and overkind person really angry underneath his "friendly" façade? Is the display of angry temper a cover for intolerable frustration? Sometimes we are not even sure of these things in ourselves. We don't know why we were curt, or withdrew from a relationship and left the other person wondering what was wrong with us.

Language cannot be dealt with apart from our understanding of commitment or apart from the total life-style by which we function. In fact, language is but a continuation of the "way we are" in our intrapersonal behavior. The person whose inner life is immune to the strength and guidance of God's spirit can hardly be expected to display a spirit of community in his overt acts. However, it is also true that expressive acts can be the means of bringing about changes in ourselves. The errors and frustrations of our encounter with others can easily remind us of the inadequacies within ourselves and cause us to change within. Language, therefore, is not only a final step in the process, but also the opportunity to test the entire range of our style of life.

I

Of all forms of human expression, speech is the most obvious and the most frequently used. It is the most pervasive of all our capacities. It can travel through walls and around corners and, under favorable circumstances, can be projected over a long distance without the aid of mechanical or electronic devices. It is capable of recording every emotion we possess. It moves people into action, even startles them; or it can stop them dead in their tracks. Speech is power even when it is not intended to be so.

The power of speech is derived mainly from the relation it has to the societies in which we live. Standards of behavior gain support from talking about them. The flow of human traffic is controlled by words like *please* and *thank you*. A cry for help is readily understood. The congregation expects to understand what the minister is saying. The exchange of words guides the most complex operations devised by society. At the same time, shared values, norms, and the division of labor are determined by the use of words. As society becomes more technical and more diverse, it depends more and more upon efficient use of words and upon the storage of information. Every era develops its own language which, in turn, assists in bringing about new eras.

How does religious language fit into our changing and pragmatic social climate? Is it useful, understood, or even necessary? The "words" of the Christian faith can and do become sterile and meaningless. They are used mainly within the walls of the sanctuary or in theological discourse. For the average person they are familiar but only partially understood; they are very difficult to get into an everyday conversation. When used in normal conversation, words like *justification, regeneration,* and *righteousness* seem almost awkward. Even the word *morality* is suspect—unless, perhaps, preceded by *new;* this word brings it within the current experience of society and hence within its fund of speech.

If the language of our faith has lost its meaning, this has not come about because the words have necessarily ceased to refer to important concepts of the faith. What once was intended by them persists as a means of understanding the demands and goals of the faith. But the words themselves have emerged from a society that could relate to them and now are being used for all aspects of its life and thought. The church often acts as though the words themselves are the truth of the faith, instead of symbols of the faith. The Word is sacred; words are not. Words are an activity through which symbols are used and interpreted. Therefore, words are useful only to the extent that they become an accurate symbol of the meanings we intend.

One pressing need in our society is to find an effective language of faith. This may require new words; more important, it certainly requires us to use the words that can clearly express our commitment and maintain communication with the world and within the community of God's people. To find this language, some basic understanding of its nature and function should be looked at.

1. *Language is learned behavior.* It is the gift of God for man's use. At the very beginning, when God created the beasts and the birds, he "brought them to the man to see what he would call them; and whatever the man called every living creature, that was its name" (Genesis 2:19). The naming process is vital for living together. If the animal is to be called a lion, it must be a lion to everyone. The word is more than descriptive; it symbolizes a beast feared by man. If someone shouts that a lion is coming down the street, the reaction would be entirely different from the reaction to the shout that the ice cream man is coming. In neither case does the person need to ponder the meaning of the words. They are so familiar that they immediately elicit a collective response.

While most of our language serves everyone equally well and provides us with the basic communication tools of living, there are languages appropriate only to special groups. The physician, the engineer, and the politician have words understood mostly within their own activities.

So do the churches. It must have seemed more convenient that way. As long as the church maintained strict and complete control over society, there was little conflict. With the coming of a pluralistic social structure, the church and the Christian face a dilemma not yet resolved. By maintaining its private language, the church tends to shut itself off from the world. On the other hand, if it speaks in the language of the world, what will happen to its private and "sacred" words?

To solve the dilemma Christians will need to learn that there is no "God language," only the language (or languages) of man. They will need to know the names people are giving to things here and now. The process of naming cannot be stopped or even slowed down. We can move, see, speak, and hear only if we engage in the naming process. There is the fear that the language of the world or a new language of faith will be inadequate to communicate the word of God. Quite so, but it is obvious that this is equally true of what we now believe to be the language of our faith. Later on we will see how the Holy Spirit transcends all language as a further answer to this dilemma.

2. *Language is the instrument of search.* Among the individual differences we manifest, one of the most apparent is the private meaning we attach to words, especially words that convey spiritual meaning. *Freedom* will mean different things to a politician, a member of the New Left, a prisoner, or to a member of an oppressed minority. *Love* will not be thought of the same way by a Hollywood producer, a newly married couple, or by a psychologist. The same could be said for a wide range of terms normally associated with our religious vocabulary: guilt, faith, joy, suffering, hope, doubt, Jesus, God—to name a few.

Moreover, it is most interesting that these terms have "leaked out" into the world. One no longer needs to go to church to hear them or to hear discussions about them.

Exactly how much credit the church can take for bringing this about is open to question, but it is significant that these terms have "escaped" from the religious community. This is probably cause for some rejoicing. Even if the words do not mean the same, at least the church is able to find common ground with the world in the words themselves.

What promises to be an opportunity for Christian communication, then, also confronts us with a most exacting challenge. The temptation remains to enter into conflict rather than search. Our "joy" is better than your "joy." Your "love" does not mean the same as our "love." We take pride in the fact that the Christian faith somehow has a priority on its words and only by reference to their established meanings can they be understood. Of course, the search for meanings has occupied the faith for many centuries, but in no age have the meanings been clear without reference to the social, political, and cultural conditions out of which the words emerged. In our world we are faced with a new dimension. In the past it was the theologians who talked to each other about the meaning of freedom, hope, and love. While this conversation continues today, secular society has asked for a voice too, so that Christians find themselves in a trilogue rather than a dialogue.

This complication should confront us with the function of language as the search for meaning. Religious education has been guilty of using language as a means of indoctrination rather than as an instrument of search. The purpose has seemed to be the eradication of doubt. If this is true, it is little wonder that we now face the task of communicating with overactive impatience and hot rebellion among our youth. All too often the strong criticism of authority figures and institutions by these persons is but a violent expression of what the church has been guilty of doing in more polite fashion. To say to another, "In love, I tell you how wrong you are" may differ not at all from just saying, "You are wrong!" In both instances words are not being used as instruments of search, but as declaration of unalterable positions.

The secular society has, in a sense, brought the church's attention to the necessity for search and has taught us something about the way it takes place. On the surface, there seems to be a cycle in which society develops a language, which in turn helps the society to change and grow. Many may feel that if only people would accept the language of the faith, the society would change; that since a small "society in the distant past" created this language, the duty of the Christian is to fit it into all societies that emerge. This has not worked. The formation of both language and society is brought about by persons who are willing to search and experiment. They give names to the things they find.

The overarching question then is: Who is doing the searching? Where can listening persons and persons committed to Christian communication be found? The language of the faith is no longer confined to an institution. It cannot be shown that the church has moved into the world with an effective witness, for there is ample proof that the life-giving and reconciliation-bringing words are "spread abroad" in the speech of an increasing number of persons. We are seeing the fulfillment of Jesus' promise that if those near him do not declare their praise and love, the very stones will take up the cry. From the most unlikely sources the language of the faith is heard. The hot rebel demonstrates for justice, the youth searches for the meaning of love and joy, the patient tells the therapist about his guilt, and the minority-group member sings about freedom.

In a volatile and diffuse society the committed Christian cannot escape the people who use these words. The search

is already under way. The Christian has only to choose
whether or not he will join in it. This raises the questions
of how well he is prepared to do it and how easily he can
carry on the search once he becomes a part of it. Not all
persons have the same degree of readiness. Many have been
completely disillusioned by the disaster which threatens
the world. They cannot see how it is normal to love in the
midst of mass prejudice, war, and human misery. In fact,
some of this doubt is in all of us. We may even believe we
should not talk about the "fruits of the spirit" when they
cannot belong to all people.

Yet it is in the center of, and because of, these circumstances that the Christian must function. He cannot retreat
into the safety of the religious community without facing
the fact that in doing so he has actually separated himself
from the community in which God is at work. The task is
massive and the results are not always obvious. For most of
us the goals of communication are limited, as in the arena
in which we must function. But regardless of the level at
which we choose to function, the commitment is exactly
the same. We are engaged in the use of religious language
as a means of forming and re-forming the community of
God's people.

3. *Language is a spiritual enterprise.* This is the case
whether we intend it or not. The commitment of the person eventually will be expressed in his language. He will
reveal the nature of his intrapersonal communication—his
view of the world, of himself, and of God. (If he is disillusioned about love, for example, he may use words to
show how ridiculous and futile love is.) This may be the
reason for the "sick" jokes and preoccupation with the gro-
tesque, which hold up to ridicule the language of traditional Christianity.

If the person is afraid, his speech will be defensive and
intolerant. Or he will be oversupportive of one group of

people as a protection against another group. Regardless of the dynamics out of which our speech develops, we can usually express those feelings within the words common to all people. The hateful person does not need a special vocabulary to express his hostility. Almost everyone will recognize words used by someone who is angry. Indeed, the number of words used in everyday life is quite small, and in many instances the same word is used to convey several meanings. Although the vocabulary used generally by people amounts to about six hundred words, the meanings they convey are limitless.

In the past we have probably made the mistake of thinking that the spirit of Christ and the will of God could better be understood by increasing the number of words used to describe them. But the multiplication of words within the vocabulary of faith will not in itself enhance the love of God. If we have to say, "Let me try to find another word for what I mean," we are inefficient witnesses to God's will. Not only is this true because of the inadequacy of words, but also because of the way we are listened to. People do not hear words as well as they do the tones of feeling. How often in committees and conferences do we hear the "right" things being said by the "wrong" person? If someone is noted for his negative and uncooperative attitudes, he is suspect. People will be more apt to listen to him and not to his words.

No language can substitute for being or for a style of living. Unless we "become" our words, there is no satisfactory communication. We can say any number of things and even feel satisfied that we have said them well, but it is another matter to be certain that we have been heard. A perceptive teacher may not be overjoyed to see his class frantically taking notes on what is being said. He may reasonably wonder whether he is only engaged in a traffic of words which can easily become jammed to the point of the student's asking him to slow down or to say the words again. Unfortunately, many people will not even do us the honor of listening to our words. They will turn us off.

If we are not to be avoided or turned off, we will need to examine our style of life at two points. The first is the mystery of our being and the discovery of who we are in the presence of the other person. It is all but futile to try to describe this mystery in words, but the Christian can understand it within the framework of the gospel and in communion with God's spirit. It is the strange opening of the person to what his words really mean. By constant reference to God's spirit we may suddenly realize how inappropriate our words are to our style of life.

A woman meets a man who appeals to her. He displays the qualities she is seeking in a person to help her rehabilitate her life after a divorce. On the second date he tells her that he has spent a number of years in prison for armed robbery. Although she has always tried to live within the spirit of a Christian faith, she finds this situation so overpowering that her immediate reaction is to cut off the relationship. The aftermath of this experience could be an understandable rationalization. Instead, she becomes acutely aware of the discrepancy between what she has done and what she believes. Even though she may have made the right decision, it has become clear to her that "I am" is sometimes a betrayal of "I say." Only the sensitive person can know the anguish of facing the mystery of selfhood.

Language and the mystery of self-before-God must eventually come together if our witness is to become effective. The Spirit bears witness in us and we are freed from the fear of ourselves. Then we are freed from the fear of others. Only our commitments to God's spirit can deliver us from a spirit of immunity to our fellowmen. Our own "safety" becomes secondary to the need for self-giving.

II

These three statements lead to the further consideration that language is symbolic. The great amount of attention given to mass communication tends to make too sharp a separation between meanings and the way people express them. We hear about language being a "path along which our meanings flow," or a mechanism by which people relate to one another. It is referred to as a message being sent or a feedback from that message. The tendency to make the separation is probably the result of the attention given to the mechanical aspects of communication. Speech and gesture are relatively easy to describe and even measure. There is so much that is common to humanity in its expressive behavior that the scientist is apt to dismiss "meaning" as something residing in the brain or in objects themselves.

Language is not merely a system of names for objects in the external environment or a designation for our human relationships. It is a creative process, a part of a communication "field" formed by the world of reality, the experiences of the individual, and the inner commitment aroused by our thinking about and our openness to the will of God. Each word and gesture is as much a part of the meaning of life as are our inner thoughts and the implications of the situations in which we find ourselves. Language performs two important functions—it *points to* meaning and at the same time *is* meaning.

Learning how to make our language consistent with our total style of life will require us to develop a system of evaluation of our language. The term *feedback* is commonly used to describe this evaluation process. However, it usually comes from someone else. Did others hear us correctly? Was our language overloaded with emotion? Were we really a part of the communication event? These and other questions are usually answered by other people as they see us in action. How much more creative it would be to build the evaluation process into our language as a self-discipline. Just as we are forced to handle our intrapersonal dialogue by testing, so we should follow the same process in our interpersonal living.

To accomplish this, there are several questions to be asked about our language and gesture.

1. *Is there a reasonable purpose in what I am saying?* It would seem that much conversation is pointless, random, and without direction. Friendly chatter might seem ridiculous to someone not participating in it. On the other hand, for those engaged in it there may be goals which are well defined and agreed upon. The neighborhood coffee-house may serve the useful purpose of strengthening community ties and enabling neighbors to share common concerns. Likewise, offhand greetings and handshakes are society's ways of "keeping in touch"—a worthy goal, even though we don't usually think about it in this way. In fact, our random, unplanned speech is more goal-oriented than we realize.

When we get into prolonged and serious conversation our goals become even more important. Suppose I am in a meeting to discuss how the church can give support to a fair-housing ordinance. After the subject has been dealt with I decide to make a little speech. I speak slowly and sincerely; I punctuate my phrases with appropriate gestures. "I don't think this plan will work. No matter what the city commission does, it is the real-estate people who give us all the trouble. It would be a lot better if we could go directly to the realtors and try to convince them they should be fair in selling property. These men come to our churches and we could talk to them about this. I don't think we can legislate on such an important matter."

On the surface this seems like an honest statement of opinion, a position one could maintain with some degree of Christian virtue. But I know that the true purpose of my speech was not in what I was saying; it was in what I did *not* say. My goal, which was well shielded, was to do something about my negative feelings toward blacks. I could not say this outright, but I hoped I could achieve my goal by saying something directed toward another, less offensive goal. As for myself, I am out of communication for just as long as I hide behind language that doesn't quite express my underlying goals.

Suppose you are in this group and hear me make my little speech. You are smart enough to guess that behind my words lies racial prejudice. You certainly can't reply to my prejudice (and even if you did, I'd deny it) because I haven't said anything about that. So, you try to answer me by arguing against what I said. Both you and I develop a little support for our positions. In the end a vote is taken, and by a close margin it is decided to support the ordinance. The church has gone on record as being in favor of integration and social progress.

Someone has said that parliamentary procedure was never meant for a Christian fellowship. The incident I have just described is probably the reason why. Because I was not honest enough to express my goal in what I was saying, the entire discussion may well have failed in its mission of healing. If the vote had gone the other way, the overtone of prejudice would have been more obvious; but in either case the personal goals were not dealt with. I went away unhelped, but it was probably my own fault. If I could have said frankly that I was unable to support anything that would integrate the races, the discussion would have taken a different turn. Whatever else might have happened, I would have followed a consistent path from meaning to language. My "field" would have been intact.

One of the goals of group process is to encourage the free expression of feeling. One might question the wisdom of this since our control system is just as important as our expressive behavior. However, our feelings do represent a personal goal. We may choose to express them or not, but if we do, our forms of expression should be a true expression of how we feel and what we mean.

2. *Am I being clear?* Not necessarily right, but clear. There is a great deal of pressure on us to be right and proper, and in order to achieve these ends often we surrender clarity. This is especially true of communication carried on in the church. Both pulpit and pew have developed a vocabulary filled with obscurant symbols that point to significant truths. "Trust in the Lord," "Jesus saves," "The truth will set you free," "Love thy neighbor" are but a few of the powerful symbols containing redemptive and releasing truth. All too often, however, the symbols are inadequate expressions of the purposes they are supposed to serve. Within the Christian community the symbols form a sort of "in" language holding the adherents together. Familiar words and phrases are passed around much like the secret codes of a fraternity or lodge. Even if the intentions of the symbols are not clear, the faithful obtain comfort from the sharing of language.

When the Christian communicates with the world, however, the deficiency of "church language" becomes quite apparent. People are bound to ask what the symbols refer to. What do they mean? How are they related to what they know and feel about themselves and their world? If the Christian is able to make a response at all, it usually comes out as a listing of additional symbols whose meanings are equally obscure. An important study of the response to radio and television programs in a New England city showed that most people carried over from their childhood a religious language which they liked to hear on the religious programs they listened to. On the other hand, those who were not familiar with the language found the same programs meaningless and even offensive. This could explain our gross failure to communicate religious truths to persons under thirty. They do not recognize the symbols, let alone the meanings they are to convey. If we accuse the world of being morally and spiritually depraved, it is because their need for "bread" has been met by symbolic "stones."

The gospel is made clear only in living, and communication is an act of living. It is a discipline grounded in values that can be expressed supremely in the way we conduct all our affairs, and not merely in the way we talk about them. The Christian who sets out to talk about the freedom Christ brings cannot be intrusive or dominating. He cannot deny freedom in the act of talking about it, nor can he communicate the love of God in an unloving way. And he cannot communicate God's saving grace through a dialogue in which security and acceptance are not felt.

Sometimes we ask, "Do I make myself clear?" This is another way of asking, "Do my symbols make sense?" This will depend on whether they point to a meaning understood by all persons involved or, as Martin Buber puts it, whether we sit on a "solitary seat." We are "made clear" by the totality of our being. Language cannot forever hide the subtle nonverbal nature of our lives. Gesture, bodily movement, eye contact, and mood must also reflect our commitment. A harshly pointed finger can result in as much resentment as a harsh word. Tensions and aggressiveness come through as surely as our words. Over a long period of time we cannot help but become transparent to one another. A little experiment will demonstrate this. When watching a performer on television, turn off the sound and try to determine what he is communicating from his nonverbal expressions. Without the words to distract us, our attention will be drawn to the actor's mood, his uncertainty, his joy, or his anger.

Persons may not share the same vocabulary or attach similar meanings to the same words, but they do understand the style in which they relate to one another. We have consistently developed symbolic terms for the "way people are." If one is described as "square" or "uptight," something is being said about style. The term *hippie* might bring to mind a type of person, and we even use the word in talking about "Establishment types," "political types," or a "tourist type." Herein lies the secret of clarity in communication. Unless we are "typical" of the language, words fail us. Commitment to a vocabulary, a scripture, hymns, or prayer is not adequate. The whole man is the message, and if the gospel has not found its way into the fabric of life it will not be carried to the world through any number of "religious-type" words.

3. *Do I take time?* In all societies communication is related to time and effort. In Morse Code the letters used most frequently are expressed by the signs requiring the least time and effort. There was a period in which the news was broadcast by the town crier. Newspapers, radio, and television now give each family its own private crier. Where people are illiterate, someone reads the news to them. Sometimes radio gives the headline news. Newspapers can give more details. Smoke signals, drums, messengers, and the mail are types of communication which at times have been thought to be the optimum way of getting messages from one place to another.

So the term *media* comes into being. It is a way of describing the channels through which communication flows. Some media, such as radio and television, are fast. At any moment we can be in touch with any part of the earth, outer space, and even the moon. Some media are slow. It takes more time to print and distribute a newspaper or book, and longer to read. Communication of the gospel has used all these with astounding success. They have established inspiration for the faithful and guidelines for the unfaithful. In addition, we spend about 15 percent of our free time "plugged in" to entertainment and news, much of it offering escape from our frustrations and pressures.

That we need to escape should not be cause for concern. However, two by-products have made us wonder whether our need to escape has not carried us into dangerous habits. First, we have become addicted to low-grade and even immoral entertainment that has dulled our sensitivities. Almost anything on television fascinates us to the point where we cease to discriminate or worry too much about the quality of what we are watching. Second, because religious broadcasts and writing are able to reach so many people, our own personal efforts at communicating the gospel seem useless and even irrelevant. If communication of the gospel means to "spread the word," certainly it can be done much better and faster through channels that reach the multitudes all at once.

The amount of communication carried on by persons in the normal course of everyday living is immeasurable. The exchange of words and meanings involves all persons in a responsible dialogue where we can take the time necessary for the transmission of all facets of our selfhood. Every encounter has its own quality. We need to learn what channels to use, what is expected, and how much time it will take. Even so, we will not be able to influence great numbers of people. Love and concern generally require numerous and extended encounters to be effective. But it is precisely within these situations—one-to-one relationships, the family, the small group—that we have the greatest opportunity to establish a community of God's people.

We must take time to find the words and meanings that can be shared. Even when people use words like joy, love, peace, faith, and doubt, we cannot be certain they understand them to hold the same meaning. To one person joy may mean a temporary pleasure, to another lasting happiness. Love may mean erotic satisfaction or deep sharing of all human gifts. But to communicate we must know, and really to know takes time. At this level, argument is useless and even harmful. It requires patience to let another person say what things mean to him. If our differences are so glaring, we want to set him right immediately; but by doing so, we set up an immunity to further communication.

An example of how it takes time to find shared meanings cropped up at a meeting where four couples were discussing the problems of their marriages.

Joe: So after the kids didn't listen the second time my wife told them to stop what they were doing, I just went out there and hauled them in the house and told them to go to bed. That put an end to that.

Gloria: That's the trouble with you, Joe, you're not sensitive.

Joe: Sure I'm sensitive, as sensitive as anyone here. Ask my wife, she'll tell you.

Gloria: But you don't act in a sensitive way. If you did, you wouldn't have handled the children that way.

Joe: I did what was right for the kids. If that isn't being sensitive, I don't know what is.

Gloria: I don't mean you don't love your children. That isn't what I mean by being sensitive.

Joe: What do you mean?

Gloria: Well, it seems that you always act before you know what's going on. You didn't think to ask what the trouble was or whether you could help. You just barged in and took over just because you were annoyed, I suppose.

Joe: Well, you might be right there, but that isn't what I thought being sensitive meant. I thought you meant I didn't love my kids.

It takes time also to bring our meanings under an ultimate judgment. God is always communicating in every human relationship. In a recent work[1] Kyle Haselden points out that in the Bible the dialogue of words rises to such high levels that the word *communication* has to give way to the word *communion*. God is in communion with man, every man, in his inner being. When our communication finds the level of acceptance, openness, and freedom, God can speak. It is his spirit that convinces, judges, and educates. In some situations this can happen quickly, in others it may take a long time, and in still others it may never happen. But in every situation there is an appropriate way to act, to speak, and to listen. We can do no more. The intrapersonal activity with God must do the rest.

In the next session of the therapy group mentioned above, Joe started the conversation by talking directly to Gloria.

Joe: You got me upset last week.

Gloria: Yeah, I thought about it afterwards and I was sure you were mad at me.

Joe: I guess I was a little angry and on the way home my wife said, "You know, she's right, Joe." That didn't make me feel any better.

Gloria: Well, here we are again. Do you want to talk about it some more?

Joe: No, I think I can work it out. A couple times this week I caught myself doing the same thing. I guess I do act before I think. I don't mean to but that's the way I've always been. But I can work it out. I'll count to ten.

4. *Do I understand how others are responding?* Just as our style and words are felt by others, so we will feel similar responses in others. This does not always turn out to be what we expect. Even when we have been clear and have

1. Kyle Haselden, *Morality and the Mass Media* (Nashville: The Broadman Press, 1968).

taken time to let communication be effective, we still might not be effective. But this is not the point. Freedom demands that each person be permitted to put into his own language (decode) what he experiences and deal with it in his own inner life. Yet there is a point beyond which we cannot go. If we detect reluctance or resistance, becoming more aggressive in an attempt to convince will only cause the communication to break down.

People usually enjoy conversation, especially if they can become active in the relationship. If one person in the process is active and the other passive, the encounter is not creative. From all interpersonal disciplines we learn the importance of active participation in relationships. The teacher is more effective when the student wants to learn. The therapist is most helpful when the patient takes responsibility for helping. Preaching is most effective when the congregation is involved. This is sometimes called feedback. It is not an evaluation of what has taken place when the encounter is past. Rather, it is the ongoing part of the encounter in which *each* person measures the freedom he is permitting to the other.

It is a joy to find someone begin to respond to us. This is evidence that he is reaching for community just as we are. His response might well be alien to our point of view. But if it is a free response that trusts us to accept, much has been gained. The freedom of both persons to reach for each other brings reconciliation. Community has been established. God can work to enlighten both participants. No matter how firm and sacred the beliefs of each seem to be, they cannot interfere with the movement of each into the meanings of the other. Let us suppose two persons are discussing current ecumenical trends. One of them has strong opinions in favor of the movement, the other strong feelings against. They come to the question of the uniting of the churches.

A: I just can't see this business of the churches getting together. This is going in the wrong direction.

B: Yes, I've thought a lot about that myself.

A: When the churches get so big the unique character of the denominations is destroyed. And the individual will feel lost in such a large number of people.

B: I guess there are going to be a lot of risks involved and we won't know what they are until we try something.

A: Sure there are risks—too many of them. The church is getting along and I don't see any reason to get things upset just to do the things they say they are going to do. How do we know it will be better?

B: I don't suppose we will know that until we try. You like things pretty much the way they are.

A: Well, you may be right.

B: I don't know everything about it. I guess it might be better in some things if they just don't forget the people. After all, the people are important in the church.

A: That's right.

You will recognize this conversation as not improbable in these days. You can just see A asking for an argument. B could have responded by listing all the values of church union and make a good case for himself. Instead, he reached out at a point of common activity ("thinking about it"). In each of A's statements the way was open for argument. By resisting this trap in all his responses, B certainly must have drawn A closer to him. The problem of uniting churches was not settled, but both A and B did succeed in establishing between themselves the kind of understanding necessary for the churches if they ever do unite.

5. *What next?* To some degree, most of our relationships persist. The same people move in and out of our lives at regular intervals. Some of them we see each day, others less frequently; but with most of our encounters, there is a "next time." When it arrives, we are apt to go through the

formalities of a health examination and start on random topics of current importance or a review of unusual personal experiences.

Maintaining community is as important as building it. If we just roam from one subject to another in our casual meetings, we may be doing nothing more than "keeping in touch" with each other and being polite in the performance of our duties. How encouraging it is, then, to have someone say, "You know, I've been thinking about this matter we talked about the other day." You immediately recognize that you were being thought about. The earlier encounter had sent him back into his own meanings to continue the dialogue. Now he wants to pick it up again. The bonds of community are becoming stronger, and by continuing the dialogue each person becomes more aware of what each means to the other.

The goal of the Christian is to enter the practice (lifestyle) of community. It is his constant commitment. Not all dialogue will turn out well, nor will it always reach beyond the level of the casual. But we are always free enough to permit others to find a sense of oneness with us. It may even mean that we move from dialogue to action, to the expansion of community, and to a corporate witness in the world.

Chapter V

COMMITMENT
AND CONFLICT

Communication takes place within the framework of community and serves to strengthen community. This may conjure up a picture of people living in harmony "where never is heard a discouraging word." To be sure, there is something satisfying in being able to exchange ideas and feelings freely. One might even be "improved" by creative dialogue with another. "It was a good discussion," or "we had a nice chat," we say. But if we leave it at that, communication becomes only a means of developing closed and comforting relationships. Even to understand, to appreciate, and to support, important as they are, only serve to provide a basis for action. If the church has become a self-contained and self-enhancing system, the fault might lie in its tendency to cut off the process of communication before its work has been completed.

Earlier it was said that society develops its language and symbols as the need for them arises. It is also true that language is used to shape things in the society and to organize the surroundings. If the social environment is disorderly and mismanaged, the causes could well lie in faulty notions about the nature of community and communication. Generally, the fault does not lie in the avowed purposes of man himself. He loudly proclaims that he has in mind the welfare of persons. (If he doesn't proclaim it, he at least assumes it.) This is true even when the results of his efforts would imply that he has another purpose in mind. Somehow he is led to believe that the carnage of war will make the lives of people more secure. The unjust distribution of goods among people is defended as a means of eventually providing the "best" for human life.

But something has gone wrong. The mills that produce steel to build our cities pollute our water and air. The chemicals that enhance the growth of crops kill off wildlife and injure humans. Any invention to benefit society is also a risk to society's welfare and freedom. Even the eyeglasses which improve a man's vision are a minor obstruction when he's kissing his girl. The motorcar provides us with greater mobility but hinders our breathing. The mass communication that opens our world to us at the same time causes us to gain our significant impressions from people we do not know, to make pacts with people we do not see, and to learn from people to whom we cannot respond.

Disturbances within the environment and within our social attitudes are by no means the only conflicts man faces. He must face a constant struggle in his group relationships. At no point is the absence of community more strikingly demonstrated. Nearly every person in our society belongs to an "in" group *and* an "out" group. One can no longer take comfort from the fact that he is in the majority. Minorities have finally come to give majorities the feeling of being "out." The result has been the grave awareness that in spite of our progress in communication skills we are not a community. This brokenness is marked by sharp revolt and active impatience. If we neither agree with the forms of revolt nor find it easy to identify with those engaged in them, the thoughtful Christian should be impressed by the accuracy of their diagnosis of the current

social scene. Somehow, the primary goals of the gospel—
"to preach good news to the poor, . . . to proclaim release
to the captives, . . . recovering of sight to the blind, . . . to
set at liberty those who are oppressed, . . . to proclaim the
acceptable year of the Lord"—are far from being realized.

To say that all this could have been prevented by the
force of Christian communication may be gratuitous. In our
attempts to improve the lot of humanity we may create
numerous problems we hadn't anticipated. But in all cases
we know that our problems exist long before we are willing
to do anything about them. The comfort we derive from
our gains outweighs the discomforts they create. The breakdown of communication with minorities does not bother us
as long as we can find security within our own group.
Contamination of the environment can be tolerated if it
does not infringe on our personal health.

Only through the extension of our commitment can this
be corrected. If the search for community ends at the
boundaries of our own group affiliations, we become immune to the rest of the world. Breaking through these
social and individual barriers can be accomplished only by
changing the perception of our relation to three conflicting
roles we must assume in the practice of our faith. The conflicts are inherent to our faith; they are the raw material
out of which our communication reaches a level of community unbounded by either cult or unreasoned personal
desire.

I

Communication always occurs within the conflict of commitment to both *authority* and *obedience*. These terms are
usually dealt with at their extremes, and hence in their
most undesirable forms. Authority suggests power, prestige,
sway, rule, and sovereignty. It makes the rules, enforces
them, and punishes the offenders. We have come to be sus-

77

picious of and even to resent persons in authority. The policeman, the teacher, the political figure, the clergyman are ridiculed, made fun of, and attacked, both verbally and physically. Authority equals force, it is said, and force is alien to the healthy growth of persons.

At the other pole, obedience is having just as rough a time today, in part because of the preeminence of a psychology that stresses independence, initiative, and self-enhancement. To be obedient is to be a passive, dependent follower who courts the favor of the authority. He is a nonperson, a tool of the Establishment. We look for and even demand obedience in our children—but secretly hope they will grow up to be persons in authority. We claim obedience to the will of God but turn it into authority to cause others to obey. These attempts to solve one of these without reference to the other indicates how little we know about their purpose, both in communication and in the development of personality.

No known society is without persons in authority. They are known by many names: chieftain, shaman, or the wise elders in the community. Regardless of how they attain the status of leader, their position requires them to make decisions and give orders. The strength of the position they hold is symbolized by various rituals and customs. Among the Chaga tribe of Tanzania, children are required to give their seats to an older person who enters the hut. When they receive or give a gift, they go through a ritual of clasping their right hand with their left one. Anyone approaching a chief of the Mende tribe in Sierra Leone must bend his body, place his hands on his knees, and uncover his head. In European society one has to prepare to meet a king or the pope.

While a democratic society does not insist upon such lavish recognition of authority, the symbols of authority are still present. One may have to go through a number of secretaries to see the boss. We have words of respect for those in authority: "the Honorable So-and-So," "Dr.," "the Reverend." The people rise when the judge enters the court or when the president enters the room. However, we are not likely to associate these as much with authority as with respect for the law, for our religious beliefs, and for our superiors. Still, these gestures cannot easily be separated from the note of authority.

Obedience is not without its symbols. The symbols of authority presuppose obedience. The authority speaks, people obey. But just as some people seek authority, so others may seek obedience. This attitude is generally associated with religious commitment. The monastic orders, the call to service in the church, are the most obvious examples of obedience. All Christians recognize that they should obey the laws of God, the Ten Commandments, and the leading of the Holy Spirit. Some see themselves as "obedient servants" and so have no ambition for authority. They listen and obey; if they ever question the authority, they keep it to themselves. The feeling of being obedient is not without at least subconscious reference to authority. For many, authority and obedience are sharply divided by position and function. It is not difficult for us to recognize those in authority over us and those (if any) who should be obedient.

As a communicator of the gospel, the Christian is committed to be both authoritative and obedient. He has both a message and a mission. But these are not separate functions to be performed when they are needed. If they were, they might be dealt with as we sometimes deal with listening which is defined as what we do when we are not speaking. Rather, just as listening has been described earlier as a total response to the other person in the act of communication, so authority and obedience are a single style of witness. Because of the nature of the gospel's mission and message, every Christian is put in the position of both proclaiming and obeying the testimony of what God has done for him. If we try to separate them, our communication will not be faithful to the works of God.

No better example of this can be found than in Jesus' experience of healing a man on the sabbath and asking him to take up his pallet and walk. Since work of this kind was contrary to the law, the man was criticized; and Jesus, who had started the whole thing, was questioned by the authorities. His answer was clear. "My Father is working still and I am working." Here is stated the formula for a single style of Christian action which includes both authority and obedience. Jesus is willfully "taking charge." His pronouncement, illegal though it appeared, is a firm assertion of authority. At the same time, he is conscious of being "checked on" by the One who sent him. In other words, he was faithful.

Christians have always been conscious of and sensitive to their beliefs and creeds. From these we usually derive authority, and we ask for obedience to them. This is the purpose of the catechism and other forms of indoctrination. They contain things we should know and proclaim. Unfortunately, to many they have become the source of power rather than man's reflection upon it. Hence we communicate them without being "checked on" by the One who gave them. We have even used them to terrify people and demand obedience, to the point that if one does not obey he is in danger of reprisal from both God and the community.

What has been described here in general terms becomes relevant in our communication about the source of our faith and belief. We must expect to talk directly about religion. This should take place as naturally as we talk about business or pleasure. As much as our Christian love and concern show through our lives, they are no substitute for a straightforward discussion of the way love has come to us. So, among other things, communication is "doing theology." This sounds like a big order for persons unskilled in the discipline of theology. It is no larger an order for the lay person than it is for the professional. To be a practicing theologian (lay or professional), the Christian must keep one hand on the needs of the world and the other hand on the divine power that creates and maintains the world. It is by the authority of God that we obey.

How, then, can we be faithful to an obedient spirit and, at the same time, to the power (authority) of God? First, *the Christian must decide where he is going to stand when he talks about the words of God.* Some will stand squarely within the polity and dogma of the church, taking at face value its words and deeds as being the final answer. They cannot leave the "sacred circle," to which they feel a loyalty as well as a strong emotional attachment. Although they obey the command to go to the world, they do so with one foot anchored well within the supporting authority, hoping to draw others into it. Their language is persuasive, for they are selling a "package" of what they believe to be the ultimate act of God's wish for mankind.

Others stand in isolation. They want no one—neither God, the church, nor the creeds—looking over their shoulders. They may give lip service and even financial help to the church. But they take pride in their private opinions about God's will and their belief that creeds are unnecessary. There is a marked increase today in the number of persons taking this kind of an isolated stand. Churchmen are talking about the involvement of the laity, the maturing outlook on the mission of the church, and the priesthood of all believers. This cannot help but produce resistance to any corporate authority and encourage a "felt theology" that grows out of one's reflection upon religion.

The committed Christian asks only two questions when deciding where to stand: Where is the community? What are the works of God? The simple answer to these questions is "everywhere and everything." God is at work in all of life, and people make up community. But communities vary, as do the works of God. We find ourselves in a church-school class, a bridge club, a theater party, or on the job. We are *in* them, and obediently so. We observe the rules of relationship and conduct. We join the conversation, share ideas, and act in every way we can to reconcile persons to one another. It is to the credit of the Christian that he is found in unlikely places, with people who do not fit the stereotype of the "righteous." This is the only way to be in the world.

But being *in* the world does not necessarily mean we are *of* it, even if the particular segment of the world happens to be a church-school class or a service of worship. All forms of community as well as their rules are man-made and sustained by man. When the church sets down its regulations for belief and polity, is it really any different from a service club's setting down its rules and purposes? Does the fact that we have dedicated our creeds and services to God mean that God is in full approval? Nevertheless, the Christian must obey the call to stand within a fellowship going back thousands of years and continuing to the present. We must know and respect the "God of our fathers" as well as "our God."

The Christian is *of* God. He never stands completely anchored to the community in which he functions. An important part of him remains committed to the intrapersonal communication that raises the question of his status before God in this community. God is the source of his ultimate authority. Without breaking or damaging his contact with the community, the Christian searches for the revelation that in ages past has brought to us the belief systems within which we are now obedient.

Second, *we speak of this authority in the language of obedience.* A woman in her thirties began to raise questions about the conservative and isolated position her church was taking toward social issues. She went to speak to her minister about her concerns, saying that it was time for the congregation to examine its responsibility to the community. She was particularly interested in opening a day-care center for the children of working mothers unable to afford private care. After she had explained her concern, the conversation went like this.

Minister: But this isn't what the church was established to do. We are here to preach the gospel, not to operate a welfare program.

Woman: Yes, but this is a need here in the community. These mothers have to spend a large part of their pay to have someone take care of their children. It doesn't seem right.

Minister: I agree, it is a problem. There are many grave problems, but if the church had to solve all of them, it would not have time to do its work. We have only the command to bring the gospel to people. Anything else takes us away from this basic purpose.

Woman: But aren't we supposed to meet the needs of people—feed the hungry and all that?

Minister: Yes, of course, and this is what we want people to do. If we preach salvation through Christ, those who respond will find a way. But first things first. The church must preach the word. Only then will the hungry be fed. If we get all our people involved in programs like this, they will soon forget what the church is really for.

Woman: Well, I think something should be done and it

seems to me that since the church is not used during the week, it would be an ideal place for the women to leave their children. I don't believe God would have any objections. I know I'm not as familiar with the Bible as you are and I guess the church does have its work to do, but sometimes I wonder what a Christian is supposed to believe and do. Helping these mothers seems like a good way to be missionaries right here. I just don't know.

Minister: If you read your Bible closely enough, you will find I'm right. I know how it is to become concerned about the needs of people, but nothing can take the place of or stand in the way of the main purpose of the church.

Looking at the responses of the minister, it is easy to find the authority but hard to find an "obedient" language. By the language of obedience we mean that in the midst of our certainty we are able to raise the question of the will of God. Even if the minister had come to the same conclusion, he could have done it within a search for new and more creative insights. Authority must always presuppose the lack of it. Old conceptions do not always fit new situations. The God of our fathers met the needs of earlier days in ways that may not apply to our day.

Let's try to reconstruct this conversation, putting the minister in a position of obedience as well as authority.

Minister: This would be something very new for us, wouldn't it?

Woman: Yes, but this is a need here in the community. These mothers have to spend a large part of their pay to have someone take care of their children. It doesn't seem right.

Minister: I agree, it is a problem. It does raise a lot of questions. Are our people ready for this sort of thing? Do we have the facilities? Most of all, I guess I'm wondering whether this is what the church is supposed to be doing. We have our basic purposes just as other institutions have theirs. Would such a project take us away from our first responsibilities?

Woman: But aren't we supposed to meet the needs of people—feed the hungry and all that?

Minister: Yes, of course, and this is what makes the problem so difficult. We must do our work as a church, but we can't turn our backs on people in need. We expect Christians to work in the community to help these people, and if this isn't done, it does raise the question of what the church should do.

Woman: Well, I think something should be done and it seems to me that since the church is not being used during the week, it would be an ideal place for the women to leave their children. I don't believe God would have any objections. I know I'm not as familiar with the Bible as you are and I guess the church does have its work to do, but sometimes I wonder what a Christian is supposed to believe and do. Helping these mothers seems like a good way to be missionaries right here. I just don't know.

Minister: That's putting it about the way it is. Tell you what, give me a couple days to think about it and I'll give you a call.

As interested as we might be in the final decision, we should be even more interested in the communication process itself. The minister is holding the situation in a more healthy tension between authority he believes to be supportive and basic, and obedience to a commitment to search for the will of God in a particular situation. This comes as close as possible to being open-minded. To be open does not mean that the foundations are disregarded. It means they are always put in a perspective of need. No matter how certain we may be, Christian communication demands that in our relationships we engage others in a search for truth.

Third, *obedience means risk to authority*. The other fellow may be right. The authority we hold may be wrong. It is not hard to use authority for personal support and even pleasure. If the faith of our fathers brings happiness through our belonging to a special group, enjoying privileged status, or even obtaining economic advantage, it might be that we have already substituted these for the authority of God's will. We may even show expansive concern for others and otherwise communicate with others in unoffensive ways. But let the conversation move to the point of risk to these secure positions and obedience fails. We find it easy to communicate with blacks, but the Black Manifesto is too much of a risk. The barricades go up and we gather our forces to protect what we believe to be God's will, but what in reality is only a defense of our own holdings.

This is true also of our more intimate relationships. It doesn't take much to bring persons to the point of sharp disagreement, especially in matters of religion. In fact, we may begin to feel uneasy before that point is actually reached. If someone says, "The system supported by competition is not Christian," the reply is likely to be, "You sound like a Communist." Not being willing to risk any tampering with the things we like, the communication is allowed to degenerate into the most familiar ploy of prejudice, i.e., name-calling. Community is fractured, and we are no longer committed to the authority of God's love.

It is strange that we avoid risk when our Christian faith is built upon it. Unwillingness to trust the fundamental gospel and the work of the Holy Spirit only reinforces the fact that we often defend the works of man rather than doing the work of God. To open ourselves to others is commitment to the fact that the Holy Spirit has been busy with them as well as with us. If we raise the right questions, listen, and hold our language at a level which maintains the community, the spirit of God does its work. We risk for God's sake, trusting that if our search persists, he will reveal himself to us.

II

The second major conflict arises in our commitment to *helping* and *being helped.* The Christian's attempt to follow Christ's command to heal the sick, cleanse the leper, and set the prisoner free has created as many problems as it has solved. Whether it be in gathering together a Christmas basket for a poor family or in performing missionary tasks on foreign soil, we now know we have not fully mastered the art of helping. Good intentions have created hostility and embarrassment, disturbed communication, and even resulted in dividing the community.

The reasons for this are not hard to find. Nothing excites the emotions as much as the discovery that we are being placed in an inferior position. By the same token, nothing supports the ego quite as much as the notion of being superior or coming to believe we have something to give. Our eagerness to give is reinforced by an interpretation of the gospel that puts giving near the head of the list of Christian virtues. We are instructed to give our "body to be burned," to sacrifice, to symbolize our altruism through fasting and prayer. But the way we do these things gets us into trouble. Saint Paul recognizes that if we do not have the spirit of Christ, our giving will accomplish nothing. What he doesn't say, however, is that even if we have the spirit of Christ, we can go at the process of helping quite unskillfully. We think the process is so simple. If there is need, meet it; if a call comes, answer it. In reacting so quickly to the need for help, the necessity for communication skills and the need to search can be overlooked. To rush in may harm more than help. It is not difficult to meet a person's need and at the same time rob him of his personhood. He may be made to feel dependent and inferior or to show gratitude beyond the point of necessity.

Within every individual the need to help and to be helped must be kept in tension. Community living requires that each member both give and receive. Moreover, both of them can and should be accomplished in the same act. If we are asked to give advice, we should expect to receive something at the same time. This is made difficult by the fact that the world of the Christian is populated with many persons from whom we expect to receive very little. The sick, the aging, those in financial difficulty, and the prisoner appear to be helpless, temporarily or permanently out of action and in need of assistance. The picture becomes clear. They are weak and we are strong. Our strength should move into their weakness.

Helping is a form of communication. In fact, it may be the most delicate form of commitment. To help and at the same time maintain the spirit of Christian community requires careful attention to the processes of interaction and cooperative movement. How can this be accomplished?

First, as in all communication, helping is a shared relationship. "It is more blessed to give than to receive" hardly means that persons are divided into givers and receivers. Rather, it can be viewed as a description of cooperative action, both persons being engaged in both functions, the result being a gift to the spirit of community. Nowhere is this more obvious than in our dealing with the sick and the aging. That they are often viewed as separated from the community is shown by the terms (hospitalized, shut-in, and—in the case of mentally ill persons—"put away") used to describe them. We believe the helper must bear the entire burden of community, and the person being helped is expected only to be grateful. J. H. van den Berg describes this relationship in dealing with persons who are physically ill:

> The patient is grateful, almost by definition. The person who is about to visit a patient can catch himself depending upon this assumption; he goes to see a grateful patient. Even in advance he knows he is welcome. He can be sure to be received with open arms. This anticipation may easily put him in such a good mood that he tries to enlarge the effect: he chooses a book from his library to lend to the patient or he buys flowers or fruit. But he forgets that by doing all this he may be accommodating the atmosphere of gratitude in which he is going to be received rather than accommodating the wishes of the patient. How exhausting it is to be radiantly grateful for every piece of fruit, which has to be peeled, cut and distributed; for flowers for which there is hardly any room left; and for the book which does nothing but enlarge the heap of unwanted literature and announce the moment it has to be "gratefully" returned, though barely looked at. It can be a relief for the patient when the visitor brings him nothing, nothing at all.[1]

When one person becomes ill, needs rehabilitation, or suffers financial reverses, something happens to the whole community. All its members share the need, even though it is focused on one person. We cannot remain immune to the need we share with those it has hit most obviously. All communication should heal, reconcile, and build every person engaged in the process. When we visit the sick, we should expect the patient to be an authentic person, capable of giving. I once sat with a long-term patient on the grounds of a hospital for the mentally ill. He was mostly silent and withdrawn, and needed constant protection and care. In previous visits few words were exchanged; most of our communication was done with our eyes and with the sense of our being in each other's company.

1. J. H. van den Berg, *The Psychology of the Sickbed* (Pittsburgh: Duquesne University Press, 1966), pp. 85–86.

On this particular day our bench was near a tree whose branches were low enough to be within reach. After a period of silence, he reached up and pulled a leaf from the tree. With his other hand he took my wrist, pulled it toward him, and placed the leaf in my hand. He managed a slight grin, but his eyes gave the impression of wondering whether and how I would accept it. All I could say was, "Thank you. I like it." Even though I was functioning somewhat as a professional in the situation, the question of who was giving and who was receiving was erased because it was irrelevant. Both of us felt engaged in a common enterprise, a shared relationship. The gift was not made to each other, but to God.

Second, helping can take place only as we understand fully the nature and scope of the need. Many needs are obvious. The victims of flood, disease, accident, or famine are suddenly thrown into a position where help from the outside must arrive as soon as possible. Other more subtle needs are often judged in exactly the same way. We are quick to make judgments about what others need and react according to what we think is best. One of the major barriers to communication is our tendency to evaluate what others say and the way others appear to us.

At some time or other we have all been called upon to minister to someone in grief. If he begins to cry, we are tempted to offer support by getting them to stop. "It's all right," we say, "you have to be strong at a time like this." Such a reply can come only from someone who does not want to be drawn into the suffering of others. The relationship is controlled by the person who "knows what is good for" other people. Actually, the grief-sufferer probably needs to express his loss by crying. He indicates his need, but it is lost on the person who has already decided what is needed. In the presence of strong feelings there are two judgments, two concepts of need and two feelings causing the persons to miss each other. When help is most needed, the immunity of the helper to the one in need is great.

Social and welfare workers have long since realized that apparent needs may cover a host of deeper needs. The request for food or fuel is only the beginning of the relationship the welfare worker establishes with the person seeking help. Are there other needs? Has this present crisis been caused by a deeper need which, if corrected, would prevent the crisis from recurring? The counselor knows that people seldom begin a conversation by talking about the things that are really bothering them. Only when they feel a sense of trust and the assurance that their personhood will not suffer are they free to talk about their real need.

This simply means that the person himself is best suited to say what his needs are. The Christian is therefore committed to a style of communication that will explore needs just as the same style is used to explore ideas. Above all, the feeling of community must be maintained. It is a good guess that at Thanksgiving, Christmas, and other special occasions, the churches provide help for thousands of people who will never share in the church's life. Such persons are not asked what they need, and so they cannot feel related to others who also have needs. Above all, giving and receiving are a matter of listening and understanding. We must learn to do more than understand *about* a person. He must become a part of our life so that he feels we are doing something *with* him and not *to* him. Whatever else is given, the most important gift is self-respect.

This brings us to the third criterion for helping. It should be contractual. Communication is reciprocal action in every situation. All persons engaged in it need to feel they belong, and this sense of belonging depends on how much they feel they can give, can be creative, and can otherwise maintain self-esteem. When a person needs help, he runs the risk of losing all this. People want to relieve him of responsibility, show pity, and offer advice. No person or community should ever be judged by the problems they have, but only by the way they meet them.

For most of us it is not possible to help many people directly, and those we do help should be kept in constant relationship. Otherwise, there is little or no possibility of working out a contract. Such a contract is something more than a "You scratch my back, I'll scratch yours" agreement. Rather, it is the subtle way we help the person participate in meeting his own need. If the community is built on love and Christian concern, it will see the need of each member as being the need of the whole group.

The contract to help is an agreement within the community to let each member be himself and participate freely in setting the goals and in taking action to meet them. The question "What can *I* do?" should never be asked until the persons in the encounter have asked, "What can *we* do?" Once this question is raised, the person needing help is likely to find himself in a much better situation.

A twenty-one-year-old college junior came to her parents with the news that she was two months pregnant. In addition to seeing their high hopes for their daughter disappear, the parents could see the damage this would bring to their self-esteem, prestige, and reputation in the community. The father was especially distraught and finally had to share his problem with a trusted friend. After hearing the story, the friend simply said, "Well, what are we going to do about that?" No sympathy, no condescending assurances, no listing of the many others to whom this had happened, no advice!

The father was somewhat unprepared for such a direct response, but it started a conversation that was to begin the process of redemption and reconciliation. He replied, "What do you mean, what are *we* going to do? It's my problem."

92

"I suppose it is, but if you would spread it around a bit it might help. After all, she means a lot to all of us."

"I guess you're right. What do you think I should do?" the father asked.

"Well, you have an advantage there. You must have been thinking about a lot of things to do."

The father then mentioned all the alternatives they had considered. By the time he had finished, he recognized the value and meaning of community concern. Help was available, not only to clarify the possible courses of action, but also to demonstrate that the greatest help is to learn that the Christian community can bear the burden of the single person. All its members both give and receive.

Among the problems to be resolved in communication, one of the most important for the church is the conflict between teaching and learning. Some years ago Carl Rogers wrote of his personal feelings about teaching, stating some radical opinions which he said had caused him to lose interest in teaching. To him, teaching was either unimportant or hurtful. As soon as we try to communicate our experiences to others, the results are inconsequential. Teaching is futile, he thought, but learning is productive when it is related to our own experiences and uncertainties and when it significantly influences behavior.

An opinion such as this strikes hard at the church. From biblical injunction down to the current massive expenditure of time and money on Christian education, teaching has been the church's most vigorous enterprise. However, the successes we might point to in this endeavor can be offset by the knowledge that we have not made significant progress toward the spread of God's kingdom in the world. We get tired of hearing that the church has failed, yet no amount of optimism can change the facts. Have we been teaching the wrong things? Is there something wrong with the way we go about our teaching tasks? Or is Rogers correct: do we now find ourselves engaged in a fruitless program?

As is true of giving and receiving, teaching and learning are often one-directional. In spite of improved techniques and encouragement toward increased involvement of the pupil in the learning situation, the teacher remains the controlling element in the educational life of the church The reason for this can be traced, in part, to the prevailing goals for Christian living. We want persons to be moral and virtuous rather than immoral and sinful. The path to this goal lies through a heavy thicket of biblical and theological beliefs which, if "taught" correctly, can result in an acceptable Christian style of life.

The teacher is almost certain to see himself as the custodian of these controls. His position is reinforced by the language used to describe the relation between God and man as father and son, master and servant, or king and subject. It is not difficult for the teacher to put himself in the king-father-master role. When this happens, the result is commitment to an immune relationship—persons functioning alongside one another but "safe" from each other.

Christian education has as its goal the preparation of persons for personal commitment and for useful participation in the church and world. The teacher "trains" learners to attain these goals. He brings to his task the kinds of exercises that will help create satisfactory lifelong behavior. Even when these methods make use of the pupil's immediate experiences, there is the lurking assumption that what is being done will serve some future purpose. It may not be too much to say that Christian teachers often see the future performance of the pupil as being not too different from their own. If this happens, the teacher, in addition to being the custodian of matters of the faith, also becomes the norm. The effect this has on the communication process can be disturbing, if not destructive, to the sense of community.

What about the learner? Going into a learning situation of any kind, the pupil is already conditioned to expect controls not only upon what he learns but also upon his behavior. He is prepared to receive approval ("Good" or "That's right") or disapproval ("Not so much noise," "Sit down") from the teacher. He soon learns the rules of Christian living and may find that kindness, mercy, and patience are in constant conflict with his impulses. As he grows older, he discovers these values do not fully represent the church's action in the world, so he develops a life-style in which the church is unnecessary. Or he may find his own behavior consistent with the church's controls and remain in it to further its group causes.

Although current techniques encourage the learner to take more responsibility for his own learning, he will undoubtedly see himself in an "under" position. He works to improve his position and satisfy the requirements set down either for or by the group. B. F. Skinner has made an interesting observation about education that works toward some future accomplishment. He says that in American education if you ask for salt in good French, you get an A. In France you get the salt. A parallel can be drawn for Christian education. Our concern for behavior prompts us to give approval to the learner who acts according to the prescribed virtues.

Is there an alternative? When a person enters the church, is there any way we can give him bread when he asks for it, and not substitute the stone of individual requirements to burden his life? If we are to experience significant growth toward a community of God's people, the educational efforts of the church will have to bear much of the burden. Moreover, we will need to see the teaching-learning process not as separate functions allocated to separate individuals, but as the conflicting functions within each person. How can this be accomplished in relation to the three areas dealt with in these chapters?

Commitment. The church has always laid stress upon the cultivation of the inner life, from which life's commitments arise. The methods of training for intrapersonal communication have never left the person completely free for self-discovered learning or self-teaching. The need to exercise some control over the direction of Christian learning has caused the church to set down the rules even for meditation. The person is encouraged to enter a relationship with something already prescribed. Thus prayer becomes a supplication to the God "out there" whose attributes are known and whose message is already anticipated. Reading devotional literature is too often a recounting of the expected virtues and a reinforcement of behavior.

Nowhere in training for the Christian life are teaching and learning more closely related. Herein lies the mystery of revelation. The individual is the sole participant. He waits upon God, whom he may never have known before. The origin and destination of the message are in the same person. Although the person cannot or should not forget his contacts with others and their experiences with God, in the most vital moments of commitment he stands alone. He has to think, to say "I wonder whether . . . ," "I think that . . . ," "It seems to me. . . ."

Time seems to work against any serious attempt to include the practice of intrapersonal communication in the schools of the church. During the one hour available each week the teacher feels a sense of comfort with a lesson plan and tasks to be performed. But it would be possible to work within a group so that experiences of mystery can be shared and expected. To say to a church-school class, "What have you been thinking about this week (or right now) ?" results only in silence—either because such a procedure is not an integral part of the curriculum or because we are not ready to lower the controls to that degree.

But this is exactly the direction and risk we must take. The appointed leader must "teach" in such a way that others will know he is searching, reaching for decisions, waiting for clearer understanding of the will of God. And he will expect the same in others. No person will be ashamed of his thoughts and feelings. Since the greatest amount of self-discovery takes place outside the walls of the sanctuary, the members of the group can be encouraged to write down what they think about (not what they did) during the week. The results could be surprising. We would hear such things as, "I don't really think God cares about me as an individual," "I must decide how much I am going to trust people," "Do my children really love me?" "God creates and man destroys," "Do we ever reach the point of understanding clearly the meaning of Jesus?"

Worship is commitment, not to do something, but to the search for something to do. During a Sunday service of worship one small congregation was to walk about the sanctuary in silence, each person by himself. They were encouraged to look at and touch the windows, stand before the altar, kneel if they wished, touch another person, leaf through the Bible or a hymnbook. The main purpose was to search, to be awakened, to open oneself to mystery. If people can be encouraged to learn the art of intrapersonal communication within the context of the church's life, it will be a much shorter step to the search for commitment in all of life.

Communication. It has been said that our deepest self-discovery and convictions cannot be communicated. But we try. The church has used countless symbols in its attempt to describe its deepest meanings. Tillich maintains that our most important symbols cannot be created intentionally. They grow, he says, out of the unconscious meanings we give to life. Moreover, symbols are at best inadequate and imperfect teaching and learning instruments. The educational task, however, must deal with them and take time to get as close to the meanings as possible.

In any communication event each person is engaged in both learning and teaching—learning what the symbols of the other person point to, teaching the meaning of his own symbols. In one church-school group the teacher asked senior high students to tell what comes to their minds when they think of the word *love*. Most of the answers were traditional, but one boy said, "A frog." The teacher thought this was ridiculous and made the mistake of saying so. She assumed he was only being funny or playing a game. However, the incident affected the rest of the group in another way. They were dismayed that the teacher turned him off so fast, but they were even more concerned with the fact that he was trying to express a meaning which could have taught them something.

Communication of meaning takes time. The educational work of the church almost always moves too rapidly. Time is required not only to explore individual meanings, but also to probe the meanings of biblical and Christian thought. The writers of the Gospels and the Epistles were dealing with "sighs too deep for words." Although our symbols are weak, we are further encouraged by Paul when he says that "the Spirit helps us in our weakness" and that the same Spirit "intercedes for the saints according to the will of God" (Romans 8:26–27).

Community. There are certain standards by which a good community can be judged. If its members are involved in creative and meaningful tasks, if each person is the focus of common concern, and if the structure permits complete and vital participation, we say the community is good. Some things are harder to detect, however. One of them is the way in which the community assumes its task of being both teacher and learner. We are instructed to go teach. Somewhere the church should have heard someone say, "Go learn." To see ourselves only as teachers denies both us and others access to the spirit of God as it works in all the world.

On the whole, we have not taken our learning tasks seriously. We have moved so far as to explore needs and to understand the ways of other people, but this is almost always preliminary to the final goal, which is to teach. It is the thing we hold behind our backs, the cause to which we are finally dedicated. Our training seminars for churchmen could profit greatly by courses on "How to Learn," but the emphasis seems to rest upon our development of the art of teaching.

The only true community of God's people is a community of search. We do not develop our plan of attack and take it into the lives of others. Rather, by trusting that God has already been at work in places we have not been we move into the lives of others, knowing that we have community, but also knowing that we are also still searching for it. We can only teach community by learning it through experience. To teach and learn within a closed system where we reinforce only the trusted folkways and beliefs is not enough. The commitment to Christian communication sets us off on an endless journey into all the world. It is both mission and quest, teaching and learning, giving and receiving. Only then can we pray, with conviction, "Thy kingdom come."

Chapter VI

COMMITMENT TO
THE WORLD

For most people, commitment and communication occur routinely in familiar and intimate situations. A diary of our activities would show that the persons and groups we deal with hardly differ from one week to another. We are conditioned to follow paths that involve us in the least threatening experiences. Beyond these paths, however, there are large and powerful groups to which we also belong. Membership in these groups is essentially symbolic rather than physical. Although we are citizens of a country, our physical contacts are restricted to very few of its citizens. The symbols and rituals of our nation hold us together and make us aware of our citizenship. We belong to many such "reference" groups—religious denomination, middle class, scientist, Negro, service organization—all of them supported by symbols we are expected to understand.

How does the Christian communicate within groups where he has limited physical contact? How can he be committed within large segments of society whose total workings he understands only vaguely?

There are three problems confronting the Christian as a member of a multigroup society. First, as a citizen, worker, neighbor, parent, and mate he is not in a position to withdraw from this social arrangement. He will of necessity belong to many groups, some of them important to him *because* of his Christian commitment. He cannot be a citizen *in general* or *just a parent* without belonging to a much larger group of persons like himself. Membership in groups symbolizes his membership in the community of man. There is no other way to demonstrate his concern for the community in which he lives. He must then learn the language of his groups, and if his associations are sufficiently intense, he cannot easily prevent his identification with their value systems. Indeed, because some of these value systems may seem to him to be similar to those he learned in his religious training, he readily accepts the fact that his group membership is but the extension of his church. He may even seek out those groups—lodges, service organizations, welfare groups—whose purposes and practices are quasi religious. More often than not, without his knowing it he has developed a spiritual style of life he calls Christian which is in reality an eclectic value system whose components are drawn from his several groups.

In the second place, his membership in the church tends to raise the problem of the meaning of the church itself. As indicated above, as a cultural subgroup the church is a sprawling abstraction that he cannot fully understand. He can understand only the demands for support, belief, and ritual made upon him by his own parish, but his view of the church as a whole is probably not consistent with these demands. If he belongs to a rather affluent parish, he may see the whole church as being either affluent or economically disadvantaged. If his parish tends to be conservative, he may say that the church across the world is either conservative or liberal. He may be quite familiar with the ritual he observes from Sunday to Sunday, but he knows that there are other rituals in the church unfamiliar to him. In fact, it is not too extreme to say that hardly anything the average parishioner experiences in the specific practice of his faith will give him a clear understanding of the church in the world. What is the church to such a person —indeed, to all of us? When we are told that the church must speak to the world, do we speak out of our concept of the unfamiliar "church in general"? The problem here for the Christian, then, is to know the meaning of his primary spiritual group. What is its true language? What is the nature of its dialogue in the world? This dilemma is usually solved by avoiding the demands of the "church in the world" and accepting the parochial demands as the criteria for communication with the world.

In the third place, we are faced with the crucial question of our commitment to and communication both within and across the boundaries of our social structures. How can we carry on a common search for God's will and at the same time maintain our identification with our reference group? If one listens to the voices of revolutionary unrest, it is not difficult to detect a broad condemnation of our organized systems of community, including the church. To those active in the revolt, the church is not viewed as a viable source for the recovery of one's soul or the redemption of one's life. The church is looked upon as standing with and offering no more redemption than all other institutions against which the revolt is directed—government, industry, social welfare, and education. Even if we neither agree with the forms the revolt has taken nor find it easy to identify with the persons engaged in it, the thoughtful Christian should at least be impressed by the accuracy of their diagnosis. If the Christian is beguiled into feeling that all his group allegiances are but an extension of the church, it is only a short step to the conclusion that there is not a great deal of difference between his service organization, business, or school and his church. He says, in fact, that he runs his business on religious principles, just as the church is "run"

on religious principles. Where, then, is the uniqueness of
the church as the body of Christ, the training ground for
the development of the spiritual dialogue that builds the
broader community of God's people?

To deal with these problems the Christian will need to
bring about significant changes in the nature of his commitment and in his style of communication. Change in one's
commitment to persons and situations other than those
familiar to him comes about only with difficulty, because
mankind has always established a bond between the individual and his protecting community. In the church, con-
firmation is a reciprocal action. The individual says, "I am
one of you," and the church says, "You are one of us."
These bonds are so strong and rigid that the thought of
breaking them can create considerable anxiety. A person
may passionately object to having his name removed from
a church roll even though he has not participated in years.

To evaluate or question the operation of the church
frequently meets with disapproval. Even if a local parish is
aware of changes being made in the world and in the
church's message to it, there is great reluctance to deviate
from tried and tested patterns. The individual then must
decide how and where he will witness to his faith. Will he
stay within the structure? Will he separate himself? Will
he maintain contact with both structure and world as a
witness to both of them as to what each one means? Each
of his choices may mean a special kind of communication.

I

If he stays within the structure, his commitment to it
takes the form of a persistent pressure upon people to
examine the possibility that what is called loyalty is nothing
more than "immunity" to everything that cannot meet the
conditions of the structure. The immunity is best symbol-

ized by unique forms of communication with a special language, and unique value systems that may even carry with them elaborate initiation rites. This unique form of communication keeps the group together, establishes its value systems, and sets its goals. Without it, the organization cannot exist. Even when membership in the group is scattered around the world, rapid communication helps the individual member feel a sense of belonging. The individual might not even feel the total impact of the group to which he belongs, but a limited geographical experience with it and his stereotyped conception of what it means helps him to feel a part of it. This is exactly where the person stands when he thinks of himself as a Christian. He is a member of a group he cannot fully understand except in an abstract sense. This will usually force him to intensify his adherence to the symbols and defend them against change.

If we want change to occur, we need not look for help beyond the patterns already existing in the structure. Worship, education, fellowship, and service have for centuries been the channels for knowing and doing the will of God. But these channels must not be used simply as tools for reinforcing existing bias and practice. They must be the means of search for the will and word of God in this day. Both intrapersonal and interpersonal activity within the church awakens it to the fundamental purpose of its existence—to heal, to search for justice, to plead the case of the poor, to strive for righteousness and honesty in all social systems. This means the development of a new interest in the biblical record and in the work of the early Christians. It requires a thorough examination of what it means to be God's people. It must draw people away from their status as spectators and self-servers to immerse them in an honest search for their mission to the world.

The Roman Catholic Church has been alerted to the need for such change through the work of the Second Vatican Council. Father Josef Jungmann makes one interesting suggestion as to how worship can be used to bring about this change:

> For a start, something ought to happen so that the people of God may be not just actually assembled, but become aware of having been brought together by God. To some extent this is achieved by the mere fact of being together in the house of God. It is fully achieved if God stands at the beginning of the celebration as the one who invites. From the beginning of time it is he who has brought the church together. Grace and redemption proceed from him, not from men. It is fitting, therefore, for the word of God, the lesson, to stand at the beginning of the assembly. The word of God might be explained and interpreted at that point. At all events, it should be able to find a reverberation in the hearts of the congregation, whether through the immediate response of an appropriate chant as we find in our Roman liturgy, in which the lesson is followed by a responsory, or by allowing a period of silence to follow, during which the word of God can sink more deeply into all hearts. But this is supposed to be an assembling for prayer, too. Having heard God's word, the congregation must be allowed to raise their voice in prayer and to present their desires and needs before God. This must be done, however, as a congregation, for the people have gathered together as a congregation, a tiny section of the people of God, reproducing in itself the structure of the whole church. . . . And so what is expressed should be the prayer of an assembled company, whether that be done by the alternation of spoken words or in periods of silence. . . . Such a plan lies, more or less clearly visible and more or less fully developed, beneath all the prayer of the church, at least insofar as the congregation is an assembly of the faithful and not simply a monastic community.[1]

Probably the last structural form the church wishes to change is its liturgy or form of worship. This would be as true of those communions with freer forms of worship as of those more liturgically minded. But no matter how great

1. Josef Jungmann, *Announcing the Word of God* (New York: Herder and Herder, 1967), pp. 155–56.

the pain or how deeply we are financially committed to the use of an expensive sanctuary, the search for more effective means of spiritual dialogue must penetrate the best protected of our structural forms. It will mean that in some instances we will need to challenge the existence of the church as a location. If the generation in revolt has chosen to search for meaning in offbeat places, then the church should carry its dialogue to similar places.

By choosing to work within the existing structure, the individual faces a long and difficult task. He will find he cannot go it alone. He may find only a few people willing to accompany him in his quest for a community of God's people. But his time and effort are spent in stimulating the church to an honest evaluation of its purpose and function. He will plead for church-school teachers who build into their task an honest critique of the status of the church before the world. If the individual is a minister in charge of a congregation, he has the great advantage of the pulpit to point toward those in the early church who loved one another, raised women to equal status, accepted slaves as spiritual equals, and loved enemies, even those who for ages had been outcast. He can point to the church's tendency to be intolerant of the heretic and defend itself against the world only to reach new levels of concern for the world and experience a re-formation of efforts and witness.

If the individual is a concerned lay person, the task may be less visible. Through small group sessions, church-school classes, and meetings of administrative bodies he encourages openness and self-acceptance. He appeals for an agenda that includes significant encounter with the world. He deliberately challenges all proposals and suggestions that have no purpose beyond the defense of existing patterns. He welcomes conflict and contradiction as an opportunity for creative dialogue.

Perhaps the most difficult task facing the individual who stays within the church's structure is to bring about change in the symbols which have outlived their usefulness. Some things, of course, cannot or should not be changed. The architecture and art forms of the church building are given; the sacraments have meaning rooted in the origins of the church. Beyond this, however, the way should be open to the introduction of new forms of art, literature, and music expressing the humanness of life and the grace of God's forgiveness to his children. Symbols of love, unity, self-awareness, human justice, and the healing of the individual and his environment should find their way into the worship, educational and communal experiences. In doing this, the church will soon find itself identifying with the needs of the world and will become more conscious of its need to communicate beyond its borders. These are some of the things that can happen when the person chooses to communicate within the structure of the church.

II

The individual may decide that working within the church's structure is impossible, or at any rate too slow a process. For him, the church is incapable of healing the world's wounds (or of even healing its own). So he begins a search for a new group affiliation. He may find another "church" or join others in the creation of a "church." If he takes this option, he faces essentially the same tasks as the person who chooses to stay within the church. To be sure, he may find it easier to reach his goals and will encounter less resistance to his proposals. Among such people there is readiness to move into the world, protest at the doors of government, awaken people with stark reminders of evil and with sharp proclamation of God's love. They will be found in the open spaces of the inner city, in coffeehouses, or on the floor of someone's "pad."

If these people are trying to find their souls and communicate the gospel, the way they go about it is astoundingly reminiscent of the way of the church in the past, of Saint Francis in the marketplace, of the early church in the catacombs or in the homes of the faithful. In our day these persons have made a sharp distinction between the church that has avoided its purpose and task and an emerging church searching for new models and symbols. But like those who stay within the church, they attempt to carry on their intrapersonal and interpersonal activity in relation to the will of God.

There are others, however, who, in an honest search for justice and peace, abandon not only the structure of the church but also its basic presuppositions and power. The gospel is bypassed. They believe that a new concept must be found to move governments and people to action. If the individual chooses this path, his patterns of communication become defensive as he seeks to create a new conceptual framework in which to operate. He becomes overcritical of existing institutions, including the church. He may take the position that only with the destruction of existing forms can social redemption occur. His protest becomes "hot," and in joining himself with others he begins to develop a "folk" religion based on hatred instead of love, exclusion instead of inclusion, immunity instead of community.

Hugh Dalziel Duncan sees the rise and fall of Hitler as a good example of the application of religious forms of Hitler's own making to a political concept and ambition. In Hitler's case it was a religion based upon race, social conflict, and war. There was no room for group decision, only the authority of a priesthood that ruled under a "divine" mandate. The authority communicated in forceful and ruthless symbols. The world was divided between good and evil persons. The evil were against him, the good were for him. There was no middle ground.

Hitler made himself a symbol. He was the image of struggle for the right. His speech was the constant rehearsal of past and present struggles against villains, and the vision of a final victory in which all the enemies would be eliminated. When the speech was finished, the authority left the scene. No argument or discussion, no dialogue with equals, no questions from the audience. Duncan summarizes Hitler's symbolic technique:

> Such then was the rhetoric of Hitler, "the rhetoric of hell," as it has been so aptly called. Through his power as orator to the masses he unified the German people, led his armies to the gates of Moscow and Cairo, and finally plunged the world into a long and terrible war. But there was one flaw in his oratorical dramaturgy. *He could not talk to equals.* After 1932, when he began the use of microphones, he heard a new voice booming over audiences now increased by many thousands in great halls. He ended by hypnotizing himself. Serious talk with staffs, searching discussion, careful weighing of issues, the ability to listen carefully to devoted followers who disagreed—all this became impossible. Soon he began to address every audience as a mass audience. The Nazi movement soon became a movement of orators. Only those who could move a mass audience to roars of applause were valued. The whole world was a stage only slightly larger than the Hofbrauhaus or the Sportpalast. At the end, when suffering and death was the lot of Hitler's Germans, he was still making speeches to masses who now existed only in his own fevered imagination. In his last weeks his only audience was himself and a few followers.[2]

It may seem too imaginative to compare the dictatorial techniques of Hitler to the methods of those who move from the church to some form of political or economic

2. Hugh Dalziel Duncan, *Communication and Social Order* (Totowa, N.J.: The Bedminster Press, 1962), p. 245.

system for solutions to society's problems. Moreover, it can be argued that there are many who stay within the bounds of the church who display the same attitudes and skills. Of course, this is true. One can gather considerable evidence of authoritarian behavior within and without the church that can lead only to the destruction of the "enemy" and to the anticipation of victory for the "righteous." But the end result of this process is the "force of speech and arms," rather than community. All forms of listening, affirming, and helping are laid aside. To search for redemptive action without the bounds of the will of God is a futile quest.

III

Earlier it was said that the Christian communicates within conflict. He stands with one foot in the certainty of his commitment and the other in his openness to new truth. He acts by the grace of God but takes risks in exploring new possibilities for service. Nowhere is this conflict more obvious than in the person who chooses to stay within the structure of the church and at the same time become a significant participant in the world. This person chooses indeed to *be* the church in the world. He is a bridge between need and mission. He brings to the church the news of the world and to the world the good news of God's love.

This person is concerned with the growth and maintenance of the community of God's people, but his primary interest lies in his movement among the structures of society outside the church. His mission is to interpret the word of God by moving significantly into the affairs of men at every level open to him. He senses the temptation to become conservative even when changes are made within the church. He is not as impressed by the "re" words often used by the church—*re*treat, *re*newal, *re*act, *re*spond, *re*hash,

etc.—as he is by the "pro" words that suggest a more aggressive attitude—*pro*claim, *pro*test, *pro*tagonist, *pro*ceed,
*pro*fess, etc. He finds his life to be an alternation between
withdrawal into the fellowship of God's people and assertiveness in the world of men and ideas. He knows he
cannot wait for the world to come to him; he must go to
the world.

Once he moves into the world, his intrapersonal communication must meet the demands of three distinct voices.
The first voice demands that he must be the church. Even
though it is ill defined and has many ills, it is the people
of God with a mission and a message. From this bedrock
of faith everything he says and does takes meaning. What
must the church say? How can the individual say it so that
it is expressed as the church would say it? He may speak as
an individual, but always with the knowledge that he cannot speak without reference to a community in which God's
love is the binding force.

The second voice demands that he be true to himself.
The church exists both in group form and in individual
form. In its group experience the church may be wrong or
incomplete; the individual's experience may be valid. But
just as the individual always speaks in reference to the
church, so he also hears God's voice as coming to the
church. In any case, he speaks as the church, even though
it means he must stand alone.

The third voice demands that the world be heard. The
issues it raises are both specific and diverse. Everyone knows
that the world needs love, food, understanding, and justice.
But the Christian does not spread these around without
concern for the specific way they should be ministered. Understanding in a labor-management struggle will not be
demonstrated in the same way it would be to a family in
poverty. Justice as a concept is meaningless until it comes
to rest in the world of people in a given situation. For the

committed Christian the world scene is always in flux. The solution to one problem may not apply to subsequent situations. He must be mobile and tentative in a world where issues and problems are unpredictable.

Even while this three-way conversation is taking place, the Christian must be ready to act. His communication becomes interpersonal. He joins a march, attends the meeting of the city commission, works for the passage of a school levy, supports a candidate for public office, and participates in an ecumenical institute. This sounds like a lot for one person to do and it probably is. It is difficult to convince some people that they cannot do everything or that nothing is worthwhile unless it is highly visible. One person solved his need to communicate with the world by becoming a chronic marcher. Under his bed he kept a large sign with only one word: UNFAIR. This could get him into any picket line that formed for almost any reason. Other people overstrive by acting in too many directions at the same time.

The principles of communicating with the world do not differ from those governing our more intimate associations. However, some special considerations are needed. First, it is important to become identified with those groups that offer the greatest possibility for effective witness to the world. The number of groups available to the individual is considerable, ranging from those that do little more than bolster his self-esteem to those designed to serve the community. Any group can become an advocate for justice and peace, and the degree to which it is ready to act in this way must be the governing criterion for the Christian's membership.

Second, sustained relation to a single group may bring greater results than frequent shifts from one group to another. Because all groups resist change, only through constant effort can the individual become an agent for change. Morever, all group affiliations gradually develop close relationships in which the communication process becomes more personal.

Third, constant effort must be maintained to keep in touch with the sources of power and the decision-makers in the society. One of the marks of a good society is the free communication between the people and those governing them. Nothing has been said here about writing as a form of communication, but its effectiveness cannot be over-rated. It can carry with it all the nuances of community: affirmation, listening, certainty, and search. We are told that legislators pay strict attention to persons who take the time to write.

Those who make decisions in our society may not be as powerful in shaping opinion as artists, musicians, actors, and Madison Avenue advertising people. These shape our thinking about money, sex, family life, and even religion. We are beguiled into believing that we cannot survive without the nostrums, trinkets, and luxuries being pushed at us. Studies have shown that we have a natural desire for only 25 percent of the things we purchase. The other 75 percent are purchased as the result of salesmanship. Meeting this power with the apparent meekness of Christian commitment sounds like an unfair match, and the Christian will find it impossible to go it alone.

In the fourth place, therefore, the individual will search for groups and movements that can make their voice heard. Probably the most important reason for the Christian to keep one foot in the world is found at this point. It is usually outside the walk of the church that the voice of judgment is heard most clearly. It is the black assembly at the foot of the Lincoln Memorial, the advocates of peace at the Pentagon, the poor assembled at the doors of government. When the forces that shape our minds lead us into the perils of materialistic and secular ways, the individual stands with others of similar commitment and shouts, "This is evil." This, too, is communication.

Fifth, the individual does not forget that he stands with one foot in the community of praise and worship. He gives thanks to God for his life and for the world. He carries on the inner dialogue of search and commitment. He receives support and reinforcement from his fellows. His presence is a reminder to the church that its message is being heard beyond its walls. There is conflict with those who cannot see the Christian as an activist in social affairs. He meets bias and even anger. But with it all, this is the assembly of those who somehow believe that the Christian faith has meaning.

Commitment to the will of God and communication with the world become the style for the Christian. He may do both of them badly, but in one way or another he does them. He must hope that his participation in life will sharpen his skills and force him to search for a clearer understanding of what God is doing in his world. He anticipates a style of life that responds instinctively to need with communication skills that develop and strengthen community in the world and in the church.